Sanctified and Set Free
My Story of Transformation from Shame to Grace

By

Marcia Ann Congdon

DEDICATION

I dedicate this book first and foremost to God, Jesus and Holy Spirit because without them, I would still be lost and broken. To my loving and amazing husband Dave; thank you for never trying to control or change me into something to fulfill your needs. Thank you for just loving me for me, and in doing so, helped me recognize my own beautiful wings so I could fly. I love you.   And to my beautiful daughter, Kaitlyn; I admire you so much! I have learned a great deal about grace by God blessing me to be your mom. Thank you for always believing in me and loving me, even when I mommied you through my brokenness. You are precious to me.

CONTENTS

ACKNOWLEDGMENTS

God is a God with great plans for us all; He see the big picture and His finished work. I recognize this today and I am so delighted with how He strategically arranged for certain woman to enter my life at certain times to plant loving seeds so that when the time came, I could receive His opening arms of grace, acceptance and love. I want to acknowledge those that represented the hands and feet of Jesus so beautifully well.

My Grandmother Rizzuto and my beautiful mom, I know you both spent many days and nights on your knees crying and praying for me and I am so grateful you loved me enough to do so. Thank you for your commitment to God and to your families to take time to pray for my heart and soul. He heard you and your prayers were answered.

Elyse O'Kane; you entered my life when I was a struggling teenager and I remember every Sunday, I could not wait to see you because you would be so excited to see me and it made me feel deeply loved. When I became pregnant at 18, you just did what you did so perfectly well, you loved me regardless of my circumstances. I always prayed that I would know the Jesus you knew and eventually I did. Thank you for your prayers, your support, encouragement and unconditional love throughout the years.

Donna Ekland and Lisa Runkle; you both popped in at a time that I needed to have friends that loved me for me. You saw past my ugliness and just loved me, even at times when I walked in such turmoil and darkness. Thank you for the Godly wisdom you continuously spoke into me with such love and compassion. I am grateful to the two of you for always demonstrating grace, kindness and mercy whether I reciprocated or not.

Donna Miller and Linda Rowe, my first small group leaders who told me "I am enough" long before I knew it. Thank you for embracing me even through I shared some of my darkness; you just loved me where I was at.

Sharleen Turley; God placed you in my life when I needed help walking my healing out, I am so grateful He chose someone with your strength, conviction, loyalty, compassion, knowledge, wisdom and patience. Thank you for demonstrating tough love when I needed it by holding me accountable and desiring the best for me. Thank you, sweet friend for your wise counsel, your friendship and for always believing in me. Thank you for seeing the gold within me and choosing to call it out so I too could see it.

Pam McCormick, thank you for taking the time to edit my transcripts with such kind words of encouragement and edification. I appreciate your guidance, wisdom and counsel throughout the process of my first book.

PREFACE

John 8:36TPT So, if the Son sets you free from sin, then become a true son and be unquestionably free!

I have discovered on this beautiful journey called life that if I chose to remain a victim to my circumstances, I remained a victim to my circumstances. If I believed I was alone and abandoned, I produced aloneness and abandonment. If I believed I was a failure or incapable of making good decisions, I would prove myself right, and my pride would keep me there in my junk believing it was always someone else's fault for the decisions I made. Somehow, little ole me remained innocent even though I was the common denominator and the leading actress in my life-story. Shame blames and I was consumed with this toxic, unpleasant emotion. I continued to produce throughout my life what I believed to be true about myself, others and life in general. These were my thoughts swirling around in my head that I had come into agreement with and in a sense, made covenants with.

As I continued throughout life choosing to believe that it was everyone else's fault and not my own; as I consumed myself with the mistakes of my past and clung to the lie(s), including that I was a sinner and my sins were unforgivable, and as I worshipped many other Gods like; sex, myself, my parents, other people's opinions of me, fantasy, my past pain and whatever recent relationship I was in; I remained broken and stuck in my junk; continuing to circle around my mountain of shame, rejection, isolation, lust, perversion, victimization and abandonment over and over again for over 3 decades. Every mountain I circled around, I created, and it wasn't until I got over myself, my pride and my past, challenged myself and chose something different to worship; *Jesus*, that permanent, life altering change occurred.

"It is not the critic who counts; not the man who points out how the strong man stumbles, or where the doer of deeds could have done them better. The credit belongs to the man who is actually in the arena, whose face is marred by dust and sweat and blood; who strives valiantly; who errs, who comes short again and again, because there is no effort without error and shortcoming; but who does actually strive to do the deeds; who knows great enthusiasms, the great devotions; who spends himself in a worthy cause; who at the best knows in the end the triumph of high achievement, and who at the worst, if he fails, at least fails while daring greatly, so that his place shall never be with those cold and timid souls who neither know victory nor defeat." Theodore Roosevelt

I absolutely love the above quote by Theodore Roosevelt and I totally get it! I have been in the arena; have fought the battle and I have many battle wounds to prove it. Now that I am healed and on the other side, tasting victory because of God's perfect redeeming love for me, I can see what worked and what did not. I am here to say that today, I rejoice and give thanks to God for my time in the arena because due to my arena time, God's glory is revealed and I write this today not as a woman with a relationship or sex addiction; consumed with shame, but as a daughter of a King completely sanctified and set free.

Throughout this book, there are a few things I do want to make clear upfront. I will not hide behind any masks, facades, religion or excuses so that I feel better about the choices I made in my past. I will not blame, shame or judge others even if they took part in my wounding because I have learned firsthand that blaming only kept me in my junk and far away from inner transformational healing. I will however in love; be open and honest, forthright and to the point; meaning what I say and saying what I mean. I am not a fan of sugar-coating unless it is on a cake or cookie. I will be vulnerable and transparent because I found that this combination opened the floodgates to breakthrough for me and birthed within me a deeper level of healing and restoration that hiding behind masks or pride never produced. In addition, I am a huge fan of getting uncomfortable because I have found that comfort always awaited me on the other side of discomfort. I have included in this book some of the challenges I myself walked through while on my inner healing journey that produced amazing results.

My heart's desire is for God's desire for you to be evident, tangible and to leap off the pages and embrace you in ways you have never experienced before. And I pray over you from *Numbers 6:22-26 – "The Lord bless you and keep you; the Lord make his face shine on you and be gracious to you; The Lord turn his face toward you and give you peace.* In Jesus name, Amen.

1 THE FOUNDATION OF OUR IDENTITY

The Importance of a Healthy and Holy Identity

Before I became fully aware and in agreement with my authentic identity; who truly defines me, my worth, value and purpose, I chose to be locked away in a prison cell of fantasy, lust, denial, perversion, self-pleasure, orphan, victim and slave mindsets, depression, fear and anger, to name a few. Why did I choose these places of residence for so long? Why did I believe that was the lifestyle best suited for me? Why did it take so long for me to permanently break free? Let's be honest and frank here, I was not literally chained up in shackles or locked away in a prison cell. I could have at any time, opened my prison cell of choice and stepped out. So why did I stay a prisoner to these mindsets and lifestyle choices for 3 decades? I'll tell you why. I stayed imprisoned there due to the hundreds of lies I believed, as truth, not only about myself and others, but God, Jesus and Holy Spirit too. *It was the lies I chose to believe that led to my life of darkness not the other way around.* It started in *my* brain, slowly traveled to contaminate *my* heart and spirit, and then was demonstrated through *my* actions. No one had me in a headlock or had a gun to my head when I made the choices I did. The same is true with inner healing, it starts in the brain, travels to the heart, *if we allow* and then can be seen with the way we live out our lives. On average, there is only 12-14 inches between the brain and your heart, but man, sometimes that short distance is rarely traveled when pride is in the way. In addition, I believed feelings were all bad, so I tried not to feel.

By the time I was 14, I had securely *anchored* myself to the following lies:

- I am dumb, dirty, bad, unworthy, incapable, a failure, different, shameful, forgotten, unlovable, not chosen, rejected and alone.
- God was a punisher, unsafe, disappointed in me and angry with me.
- It was imperative that I was pretty to be chosen, favored, loved and accepted. The prettier, the better.
- I needed a prince to ride up on his white stallion, choose me as his, love me at first sight and carry me off into the sunset in order to be happy.
- Being me was not good enough so I needed someone else to improve my existence, value and worth.
- My parents would never accept me or approve of me no matter how hard I tried.
- Love and punishment are one in the same, they both hurt and cause pain.
- Certain parts of my body are dirty.

As I grew in age, so did my lies and my desire for acceptance, approval and attention from men. While as a young teenager it seemed only natural and harmless to go steady with different boys from my school in search of my Prince who would complete my life. However, my Prince just so happened to go to a different high school, and I met him at a large amusement park instead, and between the ages of 16-18, I felt complete. What I was unaware of is that as I securely placed all my identity, value, worth and purpose in this one boy, when the relationship abruptly came to an end, so did I. I died with the relationship and remained stuck and traumatized; desperately trying to find hope and happiness again yet unaware that I never will if I continued to look for it from a man.

Since I never experienced this type of pain before, I had no idea how to process through it and my 18-year old self did the only thing she knew how to do, and began another quest for a replacement of the soulmate she just lost, so she could feel alive, have value and purpose again. This desire of mine to be accepted, loved, rescued, paid attention to and admired by a man; or in other words; worshipped, eventually developed into a relationship addiction, which then led to a sexual one. In this very long season of my life, lasting some 30 years, I destroyed the one thing I desired most as a little girl and that was to experience pure, sweet and innocent love.

It has not been an easy road this side of redemption and restoration. I would be lying to you if I said otherwise. *Stretching can be uncomfortable but is necessary for growth.* I am 56 years young and I can honestly say that 48 of those years I lived or attempted to live life from the lies I believed as truth and 30 of those 48 years, I was caught up in a whirlwind of fantasy, lust and sexual perversion. Due to these choices I made, I unknowingly destroyed my ability to connect and be intimate outside of bedsheets and in addition, I also programmed my brain to fear real intimacy and so viewed it instead as something unsafe, unpredictable and not to be trusted. My brain needed to be restored, rewired and in many cases, reprogrammed.

Change can be very uncomfortable but very necessary if we desire different outcomes to playout in our life. I knew that unless I changed inside, nothing was going to change outside.   If I continued to receive my value and worth from a horizontal source and not vertically, I was going to continue staying stuck in my junk and my physical outcomes would remain the same. I chose to get very uncomfortable and challenge myself in so many areas for the breakthrough and change to take place and become permanent and I finally loved myself and believed I was worthy of that change. *Change happens when you change. If you desire your circumstances to change, YOU need to change, not everyone else.*

As this journey for inner transformation took place, my desire for love and acceptance of man shifted to a desire and need for a deeper and more meaningful relationship with my heavenly family. My desires changed from trying to please man and myself, to desiring to only please God. My former life which involved sex, control via manipulation, a world of fantasy, lustful thinking, lewd and vulgar conduct, exhibitionism, inappropriate dressing, emotional outbursts and zero boundaries was a thing of the past and a passion to just be in connection with Jesus erupted and everything about me and my identity shifted. It is nothing short of a miracle that when I chose to become completely renewed, not only within my brain but within my heart, spirit and my soul, that my sights and desires were no longer set on things of this world but instead on Heaven. Paul says it best in *Romans 8:5 - Those who live according to the flesh have their minds set on what the flesh desires; but those who live in accordance with the Spirit have their minds set on what the Spirit desires.*

I have gratefully lived these last eight years pursuing wholeness by receiving His living water so to purify and heal every broken area within me, layer by layer, glory to glory. This time in my cocoon, has required me to die of myself over and over and over again as I willingly go through my transformation process. Even today, I am still at it and still passionate about inner transformation, inner growth and breakthrough. I am passionate about hearing from my heavenly family and coming into complete agreement with their perspective, not this worlds and that requires me dislodging rocks and in some cases boulders that had gotten in the way from the years I spent living in and from sin and shame.

- Today, I see each challenge, each rock or boulder as a gift, not a hindrance.
- Today, I no longer crave or desire a temporary high; experienced in-between bedsheets or lust-filled glances, but instead my passion is for true intimacy with Jesus and deep inner healing. My eyes stay focused on Him and Him alone.
- Today, I no longer need to people please.
- Today, I no longer have a need to entice men for pleasure or self-value; I have value and worth as a daughter of The King of Kings.
- Today, I no longer have a need to be the center of attention and dress accordingly for that to happen because God has clothed me in righteousness, and I welcome that clothing exchange.

- Today, I no longer need to fit in with the world's standards to feel worthy or adequate.
- Today, I no longer desire things of the flesh.
- Today, I no longer look upon myself from a perspective of brokenness, but from one of wholeness because that is how HE sees me.
- Today my passion is no longer lust driven but Christ driven.
- Today my Identity is no longer based in lies, my past or false and wounded perspectives of myself and others, but solely based in truth from Gods perspective only.

You see, when The God of The Universe, who created me out of perfect love says, "I have chosen you, you are mine!" *Everything* within me, which He originally created; awakens, recognizes and responds to His almighty voice. My bones, blood cells, nerve endings, tissues, chromosomes, neuro pathways, the chambers of my heart, my liver, spline, intestines, corneas, ear drums, skin, hair on my head, fingers and toes all recognized and responded to the frequency of His voice.

I had to stop agreeing with and living from the grave I dug out from the lies swirling around in my head, I chose to believe. I had to stop my stupid thinking I had partnered with for way too long, get over myself and then choose to come into agreement with what His word has always said. Why did I believe the bible was written for everyone else but not me? Oh, good grief! Like I have so much power that God decided I was excluded from His graces. Yeah, that mindset was not working out for me and that too had to change and so I gave God, Jesus and Holy Spirit permission to have their way and operate on all of me. I rose out of my grave, a bit scared and unsure, removed my grave clothes of lust, shame and rejection and tried on new garments of acceptance, worthiness and grace. At first, I was not comfortable wearing these new clothes but as time passed and I continued to speak out what God was saying about me, not the lies within my head; the discomfort I originally felt, yielded and gave way to comfort.

Isaiah 43:1NIV - But now, this is what the LORD says-- he who created you, Jacob, he who formed you, Israel: "Do not fear, for I have redeemed you; I have summoned you by name; you are mine.

2 Corinthians 5:17NIV- Therefore, if anyone is in Christ, the new creation has come: The old has gone, the new is here!

In the beginning

"Love originates first within the walls of the womb, expands to the walls within your crib and later throughout the walls of your home. Redemption occurs when you allow it to rest within the walls of Father God's heart and flow directly into yours." M.A.

Let's go back to the beginning, shall we? The day we are born into this world, we are completely helpless and dependent upon whoever our caretakers are. We enter this world knowing absolutely nothing and we begin this new journey of life, discovering things we believe as true from the perspective and behavior of our caretakers and the world played out around us. We are like sponges soaking up info along the way and this info is stored in our brain as fact because it is all we know. We trust our caretakers so why would it not be? Inside the walls of our cribs is where love and trust are originated based on how it is demonstrated to us by our caretakers. Therefore, the emotional and spiritual health of our caretakers is crucial in determining our own emotional and spiritual health. They are the ones that teach us about love, forgiveness, fairness, conflict resolution, compassion, generosity, integrity, trust and most importantly whether they believe in us, admire the person we are; our unique and authentic self with our own talents, gifting's, callings, dreams, purposes and differences. I am not a big fan of Co-dependency, mainly because to me, it is an identity and destiny destroyer and robbed me personally of many years of my life. There is no way you can become your authentic self when you have one or both parents needing you to fulfill their needs, hopes and dreams. The only thing you become from needing to fulfill your parent's needs is a people pleaser. When I say authentic, I do not mean what your parents spoke over or into you by no means. I'm referring to what God says about you and what He created you for. There is a big difference.

Every child is born with certain core needs that God placed there such as to belong, be significant, secure, loved, valued, heard and chosen. Much of an individual's identity is determined by how well these needs were met or not met. When these needs go unmet due to an unhealthy and unstable childhood environment, the *innocent* child's core needs are still there and are still unmet. Fast forward 10, 20, 30, 40, 50, 60 years, if still left unmet, recognized and dealt with, this now adolescent and eventually grown adult will have those childhood wounds and unmet needs contaminating and controlling much of his or her life choices. Just because you grew in age and size does not mean those needs disappeared. They are needs not wants and they are of value to whom and what you become; your perspective in life about yourself and others; whether you see yourself as valuable and worthy; whether you feel safe and secure or live from a place of fear; whether you are confident in your own skin or need to people please, so to be liked by others and feel of value. There is so many more areas that unmet core needs impact in our lives once we reach adulthood.

Have you ever witnessed a grown person acting like a child? That is an unmet need, not met and this adult is behaving pretty much at the age the wounding occurred. Those needs are still there inside your now adult self, crying out in a sense needing to be met, to be heard, validated, seen or understood. This now wounded adult is walking through life with their wounded inner child calling the shots, and in many cases contaminating their life and the lives around them. Trust me when I say that when I lashed out at my loved ones and friends due to my inner brokenness, they became my victims not the other way around. I might have felt like the victim but in all sense of reality, they were. I was throwing up all over them and not cleaning it up but expecting them to take responsibility and clean it up for me.

Permanent breakthrough for me happened when I was the one desiring it for me; not someone else's desire for me by leading me where they believed I needed to go so I could be saved, but my own desire to walk in freedom. *You can lead a horse to water but that does not mean he is going to drink*. That was me, I had so many people attempting to save me and it never lasted because Jesus was the one that needed to save me, not them. I finally took a chance on me because I no longer wanted to be imprisoned to my past pain, but instead passionately desired total freedom. I knew I could not fool God so I stopped blaming everyone else for my own choices and behaviors, took a very hard and at times difficult look at myself and why I was doing what I was doing, and made the adjustments necessary so change could occur. This is what I like to refer to as my time in the cocoon. I had to die of myself so many times as I allowed my heavenly counselor; Holy Spirit to guide me through those times in my life where my identity took a major hit. In many of those cases it was my core needs not met or wounded by other wounded people with unmet core needs. There is a good chance that every human being on this planet has brokenness inside them, yet we are looking to feel complete, approved of and accepted, from other wounded people who too are looking for possibly the same thing we are looking for. And if you are anything like I was and receive all your worth from what others say; you are going to end up never feeling good enough because your source of fuel is not one that will produce wholeness within you. The only one who can complete you is Jesus.

We quickly can believe so many lies about ourselves and others based on the environment(s) we live in. When we are subjected to emotional or physical abuse as a child there is an onslaught of behavioral setbacks that can occur if not properly dealt with. One of the most painful and impactful ones in my life was shame. When a child is given a dose of unhealthy shame, they begin believing the lie that everything about them is bad; their body, beliefs, emotions, dreams, behaviors, etc. I was introduced at the young age of 4 to a very unattractive couple; unhealthy shaming and her partner, fear. I immediately began believing terrible things about my body and the person I was. (To avoid assumptions, the unhealthy shaming I experienced at 4 did not involve sexual molestation).

As the birth of this toxic emotion corrupted my young innocent self, I slowly began allowing it to consume other areas of my life due to the thoughts I began believing as truth. As I grew in age, so did my fear and shame and these beasts were at times way too much for my emotionally undeveloped self to fight off. By the time I was 8, I became securely anchored to shame and its poisonous tentacles and fear never was far behind lurking to make sure I kept quiet and just did as I was asked to do.

I was 7-1/2 years old and we recently moved to Columbus, Georgia where my dad was stationed at Ft. Benning Army base. This was the first time we purchased a house off the base; well that I can remember, and I was excited to share a good size room with my twin. Out of all my bedrooms, this one, by far was my favorite. My mom took extra time and decorated our room so nice with matching wallpaper, curtains and bedspreads. I loved my room and spent hours upon hours make-believing life through my barbie dolls, taking pleasure in dressing them up and imagining my own life played out through them. It was my place of refuge, comfort and safety. It was a place where I could get away from the outside world of chaos, at times consuming the walls of the house. My young and very naïve self believed in fairy tales and so longed for her Prince to one day ride up on a white stallion and rescue her from the chaos and turmoil. I longed to be pursued and chosen like the princesses were in each of the fairy tales. Their life was dark and difficult until a charming and handsome Prince arrived and swept them off their feet, kissed them gently and that one exchange made everything disappear that was sad and broken. Oh, I almost forgot to add, "And they lived happily ever after! The End. How I longed for that in my own life. Maybe one day my Prince will come after me and choose me to be his princess forever and all my sadness will forever go away.

Like any child, I enjoyed the outdoors, so as soon as homework was complete and weather permitting; you could find me in the empty lot playing a game of softball, kickball or dodgeball with other kids in the neighborhood; swinging as high as I could possibly go on my swing set, dangerously riding my bike, or digging in my backyard in search of arrowheads, Indians might have left behind. I was fascinated by their culture and at one point, desired to be an Archeologist until I found out that the job would require me to explore dark caves where bats and spiders lived and my girlie side was like, "Heck no!" Plus being an Archaeologist required me to be smart and I am not smart, that is for sure!

My childhood play time; whether in my room or outside playing with friends brought with it the release I needed to cope with other areas of my life that were not as easy or peaceful. I was gifted in the area of athleticism, was outgoing and gregarious, had an amazing imagination and was creative, but I struggled academically.

I am a fraternal twin which means two separate eggs and sperm. My twin and I do not only look different, we have different personalities and talents too. I am an extrovert and she is an introvert. I love playing outside, and she is fine staying in and reading books. She excels academically and I do not. If you know anything about twins, you know that they are constantly compared. From the time we were born, people began comparing us and even if I have no recollection of what was said to me as an infant or toddler, I was told the stories about those comments repeatedly from my mom. I love being a twin, but I do not love always being compared and feeling inadequate in the areas she excelled in.

I can't say I was ever passionate about education due to some harsh words I received from teachers, and how I compared myself to my twin and her academic abilities and my own awareness of the difficulty I had to just memorize anything enough to make a C. I would spend hours upon hours memorizing notes for a test and the moment the test was placed in front of me, I would freeze and forget. To be honest, no one had to say anything to me about being not as smart as my twin, it was quite apparent. Let me explain....

The school we attended assigned children to classes based on their grades. My twin had classes with all the other 'A' students, and I was placed in the 'C' classes, all except one. I shared one class with my twin and that was, English. I was so excited that not only did I get to share a class with my twin, but mainly because it meant I was not completely dumb in every subject. I, Marcia Ann was not a complete loser! Well, everything was going well until we were given an assignment to memorize a poem and recite it dressed as the main character. I had never recited anything in front of a class, and I became overwhelmed by the thought of it. I did not believe I could do this without messing up since I can't memorize anything.

I decided to do a poem on a friendly ghost for two reasons; one was it seemed to be an easy poem to memorize and two, making a costume of a ghost was simple. I had a week to prepare, so diligently went after memorizing my poem; praying that when I went in front of the class, it would not all vanish from my brain. The night before, I went about cutting out eyes and a mouth for my ghost costume from an old white sheet my mom had in the linen closet. I prepared myself the best I could, but nothing could shake the nervousness I felt about going before these students I believed were so much smarter than me and recite a poem I for sure was going to botch up.

This was a time that I dreaded that my last name started with a B! I so wished that day, that it was a Z. My time came to recite my poem and I froze. Fear overtook me and I nervously asked the teacher if I could run to the restroom and change into my costume. Here, all I had to do was throw a sheet over my head, but it was as if my body was paralyzed and I was too embarrassed to do that in front of the other kids. The teacher agreed and off I went to the restroom, sheet in tow. I dashed into a stall and busted out in tears. I had never experienced an emotion like this, what was happening? I could not breathe; I was shaking all over and uncontrollably crying and I had no idea why? One thing I was sure of and that was that there was no way possible I could go in front of all those kids who would be staring at me and recite this poem. I knew I would fail, and I just couldn't fail with so many witnesses.

About 5 minutes had gone by and I heard the door open to the bathroom and my twins voice calling my name. Through my tears, I answered her and opened the door to the stall I ran to for safety. She began consoling me and encouraging me that I could do it and everything would be okay, but I knew differently so rejected her attempts. She left the bathroom and headed back to class to inform the teacher that I was not going through with my assignment. I managed to pull myself together enough to walk back into class and I believe this was the first walk of shame I took. Here I was so worried about having all eyes on me as I failed and that is what was happening without me even reciting the poem. All eyes were on me as I walked with my head down through the classroom door and to my seat. I was relieved when I heard the bell ring and I dashed out of the class and headed home for the weekend.

Thank goodness it was Friday and I had the weekend to forget the nightmare that just happened in English class and prayed the teacher and students would too. Monday came and I realized quickly that she had not, and my nightmare had a 2nd act. I was devastated to learn that I would no longer be welcomed in her class and I was now placed in the 'C' English class with all the other dumb students. How could she do that to me? Why didn't she give me another chance? Why couldn't she have asked what was wrong or encourage me to try again? Why did she give up on me so easily? She must not have believed I could do it in the first place. I was *doing so well in all the other areas; homework and tests, didn't that matter?*

With an overwhelming sense of rejection, disappointment, embarrassment and shame, I left the 'A' classroom I shared with my twin and headed down the hall to the 'C' class where once again, I experienced my 2ⁿᵈ walk of shame within a 4 day span. I slowly walked with my head down low and as I entered the class, I could feel all their eyes staring at me and I just knew they all knew too what a failure I was. I decided right then and there that I am not capable of memorizing anything or capable of doing well in school, I am a failure, a dummy, an outcast and nothing I do is good enough so why even bother trying.

I personally believed I had already dealt with the above memory since I had previously walked through many forgiveness prayers; forgiving both the teacher, school system and myself for the emotional pain I experienced that day, but apparently Holy Spirit knew something I did not by leading me back to this memory. As the memory began unfolding before me, He began explaining that just because my adult-self had believed she dealt with the outcomes that transpired that day, did not mean my younger self had which is why throughout life, I was still harassed by shame, feared failure and had an innate need for justice and to be heard. My sweet and innocent 7-1/2 year old was still within me carrying around the shame, embarrassment, rejection, humility and sense of injustice from that day and until I allowed her to process through, have a voice and choose to forgive from her 7-1/2 year old self, nothing today within my 56 year old self would change. Wow!!! Since Holy Spirit is brilliant and the best counselor there is, I chose to dive-in and go after deeper inner healing by loving on my younger self in a way I never knew was possible; but GOD!

I began this process by finding a quiet place and first took time to welcome Holy Spirit and Jesus in as I went down memory lane in my quest for inner freedom. I knew I needed their assistance, wisdom and knowledge to achieve the breakthrough I was going after. I had no idea what or how this was all going to play out, but I knew one thing for sure, they did. I sat in a posture of receiving and simply asked Jesus to lead the way. No sooner had I asked, the memory came flooding back, but there was something very different now. I was standing as I look today alongside Jesus in the little girl's restroom within my elementary school. In front of us was the stall that young Marcia Ann was inside, and I could hear her sobbing. I gently knocked on the stall door and asked if Jesus and I could speak to her. She obliged and ever so slowly, the stall door began to open, and I gazed upon my younger self slumped down weeping, scared, angry, ashamed and confused. There was a deep sense of empathy I began feeling for her and at the same time anger fueled by fear and injustice. Holy Spirit instructed me to begin apologizing to her for leaving her in the stall for all these years and so without hesitation, I did. He explained to me that by not dealing with this at the time, I had left my younger self stuck there traumatized by this emotional event and today, we were going to free her.

I began apologizing to her, not only for leaving her but forgetting about her for the last 49 years too. I showed her compassion, empathy and support. I introduced Jesus to her as well and explained how He was here for today and always. I asked her if she trusted me and if so, wanted to exit the stall, and with her head held low, shook it, Yes. I then asked if I could hug her and to my surprise, she trusted me enough to come into my arms and I felt a sense of compassion rise up within me for my sweet and innocent 7-1/2-year-old self. Holy Spirit then said to listen to what she had to say, allow her to have a voice and then validate her. It was then that my younger self began sharing with me and Jesus just how she felt at that moment. Her anxiety, feelings of inadequacy, not being good enough, being a failure, a letdown, not being heard or given a 2nd chance and how unfair treatment she believed was shown to her. I held her and just listened and then when she was finished, began validated her so that she knew that she was heard and that I did truly understand where she was coming from. There was instantly a peace that came upon the two of us at the same time and I understood why that was. I knew that as my younger self was able to have a voice, felt heard and validated, a sense of peace from within erupted and my now 56-year-old felt it. There was a shift within me that happened, and I knew that I no longer was going to be led by unmet wants and needs from that traumatic memory ever again.

Holy Spirit then said; "Ask her if she would like to leave." He explained that it still comes down to a choice and this was the time for my younger self to decide whether she wanted to stay there as a victim or leave victorious. I got to my knees so I could be eye-level with my 7-1/2-year-old self and softly asked her if she would like to say good-bye to this painful memory and start a new pathway with Jesus and me? I also encouraged her by saying that Jesus and I were here for her and she would never be alone or abandoned on this new journey. She again shook her head Yes and willingly came into my arms. I picked her up and as Jesus and I walked hand in hand out of the little girl's restroom, she waved good-bye to the pain, the shame, rejection, confusion, fear and whatever else she had owned as her identity that day.

We walked together to the 'A' English classroom and noticed her teacher standing outside. I gently asked little Marcia Ann if she had anything to say to her teacher and she began explaining to the teacher how she wished she would have given her a 2nd chance and how unfair it was for her to send her away just because she was scared that day. She also added that she forgave her and would no longer own any of the teachers pain she demonstrated and released on little Marcia Ann that day. After she forgave the teacher, we left the school building and she continued to wave good-bye to all the pain from within the walls of that school. A brand-new path appeared before us and again, I asked her if she was willing to begin walking down this new path with Jesus and I or go back into the school? Once again, it needed to be her choice. She said and this time, with her head held high; "Yes, I want to begin a new path and journey with you and Jesus."

After I learned this new and amazing inner healing tool, I began a quest alongside Jesus and Holy Spirit diving into other memories where I believed I had forgiven, but discovered I was still *stuck* in my pain so therefore, was contaminating my life still today. I was uncovering firsthand just how many of my childhood, and young adult beliefs, whether true or false formed my character which impacted the way I lived out my life. And may I add; how many other lives I contaminated due to my own inner shame and brokenness which I at times, vomited all over them.

I decided to love myself enough so to stop this contamination cycle of my life today and so I stepped into becoming uncomfortable for change to occur. *I have found that on the other side of discomfort lies comfort and that is where I want to exist.* I have found from my own inner healing process that it is the bridge between the two that most healing and transformation takes place. It's the scary, vulnerable and uncomfortable part, but the part that sifting and shifting happens. As I challenged myself to go deeper and allow my infant, toddler, preschool, school age and adolescent self to emerge; reassured her it was safe, and process through the wounds she experienced, no matter how uncomfortable, and spoke truth back into her; breakthrough and healing always manifested. Sometimes it was a small breakthrough, but many times it was huge! It seemed like the more uncomfortable I got the bigger the breakthrough.

And since Holy Sprit is so okay with getting me uncomfortable, He decided to stretch me a bit further by suggesting that I can even go back into this memory and completely change it up, if I like. He explained that as I create a new memory that produces the outcome I like; I am activating healing within. God is a God of creation and creates and recreates and has blessed our brains to do the same. I thought about it for just a second and then accepted the challenge.

I once again relaxed and got comfortable. I asked for Jesus to accompany me and slowly drifted back into the original memory, but this time I changed things up.

It was the day of my presentation and I was so excited to go in front of the class and recite my poem dressed up as the main character; a friendly ghost. I had spent all week memorizing the poem and my costume was super cute too. I was a tad nervous but had confidence in myself to do a great job.

The teacher called my name and I quickly threw my costume over my head and skipped up to the front of the class. I had butterflies in my stomach, and I was shaking a bit but took a deep breath and began reciting my poem.

I was able to remember every line and I even danced a little jig at the end in hopes the teacher might add a couple of extra points for creativity. At the very end, I took a bow and the class applauded.

And as I skipped back to my desk, I had a huge smile on my face. The End.

Holy Spirit was right! When I came out of this memory, I was smiling from ear to ear both in the natural and spiritual. My spirit and heart were dancing a jig too. There was a newfound sense of accomplishment that was released as I recreated a memory that once caused me pain but now brought accomplishment and joy. This new memory replaced the old one because God is a God of making all things new.

The bottom line in all of this is that I desperately needed to relearn how to love myself in a way that produced love within me and then around me. If I could not love all of me; the real me, then how could I possibly demonstrate the love of Jesus to anyone? There is no way I would ever be successful at any type of relationship without loving myself first. It was during this beautiful and precious cocoon time that all of this was released to me through the wisdom of The Holy Spirit and I was able to begin walking out new levels of redemption, restoration and anointing by being submissive to His promptings, trusting in The Great I AM and His transformational, powerful and perfect love demonstrated in Mary's womb, The Cross and The tomb.

G.R.A.F.T.E.D.

Grafted-In
Defined as: Something (as a piece of skin or a plant bud) that is joined to something similar so as to grow together.
It is peculiarly appropriate to olive-trees. The union thus of branches to a stem is used to illustrate the union of true believers to the true Church.

Romans 11:17-24

If some of the branches have been broken off, and you, though a wild olive shoot, have been grafted in among the others and now share in the nourishing sap from the olive root, do not consider yourself to be superior to those other branches. If you do, consider this: You do not support the root, but the root supports you. You will say then, "Branches were broken off so that I could be grafted in." Granted. But they were broken off because of unbelief, and you stand by faith. Do not be arrogant, but tremble. For if God did not spare the natural branches, he will not spare you either. Consider therefore the kindness and sternness of God: sternness to those who fell, but kindness to you, provided that you continue in his kindness. Otherwise, you also will be cut off. And if they do not persist in unbelief, they will be grafted in, for God is able to graft them in again. After all, if you were cut out of an olive tree that is wild by nature, and contrary to nature were grafted into a cultivated olive tree, how much more readily will these, the natural branches, be grafted into their own olive tree!

I want to share with you something that Holy Spirit showed me when it comes to our psychological well-being. He used the following seven (7) words, (the number 7 also means complete), *repeatedly* during this transformation process in my cocoon and I love how the 1st letter of each of these words when placed together spell out **GRAFTED.** How cool is that! *Grounded, Rooted, Anchored, Foundation, Truth, Established and Defined.* All 7 of these words play a huge role in determining the wholeness and wellness of our identity and just what, who or where we are receiving it from.

Here are the definitions for all seven (7) and what Holy Spirit showed me. *(Notice the high-lighted words)*

1. Grounded - Mentally and emotionally *stable*: admirably sensible, realistic, and unpretentious. (When we are *grounded* in His word, His *truth* (Jesus) we will experience *stability*, oneness and transcending peace. *Jeremiah 17:8ESV - He is like a tree planted by water, that sends out its roots by the stream, and does not fear when heat comes, for its leaves remain green, and is not anxious in the year of drought, for it does not cease to bear fruit."*

2. Rooted - The underground part of a *seed* plant body that *originates* usually from the hypocotyl, functions as an organ of absorption, aeration, and food storage or as a means of *anchorage and support*, and differs from a stem especially in lacking nodes, buds, and leaves. (When we are *rooted* in understanding, accepting and receiving our *originality* and who *created* us, we can and will bear beautiful fruit in our life and experience life to the fullest. Our harvest will be bountiful, and we will lack nothing). *Colossians 2:7NLT - Let your roots grow down into him, and let your lives be built on him. Then your faith will grow strong in the truth you were taught, and you will overflow with thankfulness.*

3. Anchored (v) – a. To lower an *anchor* into the water in order to stop a boat from moving forward. b. To make something or someone *stay* in one position by *fastening* him, her, or it *firmly*. (When we become *anchored* solely and souly in His *truth*, we will not be easily swayed by life's circumstances). *Hebrews 6:19 - We have this hope as an anchor for the soul, firm and steadfast. It enters the inner sanctuary behind the curtain.*

4. Foundation - In new construction foundation functions are *planned in*. A building foundation performs several functions. The three most important are to *bear the load* of the building, *anchor it* against natural forces such as earthquakes, and to isolate it from ground moisture. (Our one true foundation is God Himself – He *planned* our existence and said, "It is good." He can *bear* our entire load (burdens) and when we are *anchored in* Him, we will be safe, *secure* and spiritually well *established*). *Isaiah 28:16 - Therefore thus says the Lord GOD, "Behold, I am the one who has laid as a foundation in Zion, a stone, a tested stone, a precious cornerstone, of a sure foundation: 'Whoever believes will not be in haste.'*

5. Truth - The quality or state of being true. That which is true or in accordance with fact or reality. A fact or belief that is accepted as true. So, I believed as truth what others said to me or believed about me. I allowed and gave my power over to these people instead of being confident in the person I am regardless of my mistakes or shortcomings. My own *foundational* truth was not *grounded* or *anchored* in God's *truth* or perspective, but the perspective of what I believed or perceived as *truth* regardless if it was even true and very possibly based on presumption, or another wounded persons perspective which still does not mean it is true. This only *established* within me a source of brokenness and an inability to decipher and filter through healthy mindsets verses toxic. If I believed as *truth* that I was a failure, then that is exactly what I would become. It was no different than living on an unstable fault line, never knowing exactly when my world might come crashing down around me. I continued to be shaken and rattled in my life based on whatever my choices and circumstances were. *And don't forget, it was the lies I believed that produced the circumstances I was being shaken by. Ephesians 1:4 TPT - And he chose us to be his very own, joining us to himself even before he laid the foundation of the universe! e Because of his great love, he ordained f us, so that we would be seen as holy in his eyes with an unstained innocence.*

6. Established - Growing or **flourishing** successfully. (Allowing God to **establish** us instead of man will lead to a life of **growth** and physical, spiritual and emotional prosperity and wholeness.). **Colossians 2:6-7 – Therefore as you have received Christ Jesus the Lord, so walk in Him, having been firmly rooted and now being built up in Him and established in your faith, just as you were instructed, and overflowing with gratitude.**

7. Define – 1. state or describe exactly the nature, scope, or meaning of. 2. Mark out the boundary or limits of.
Who defines me? Who or what am I giving power to that they, it, he, she determines what I think of myself? Where and why have I placed so much importance upon them that my own life only matters if I have their approval? Every one of those questions I was personally asked by Holy Spirit as I dived into the co-dependent part of my identity which basically means that I did not see myself as separate and unique, but the basis of my identity rested in the hands of others. Back before I was set free, I was **defined** and empowered by my circumstances, how many heads I turned when walking in a room, how many men I bedded, the lies I believed, other people's opinions of me, my shame, wounds, set-backs, whether I was rejected or felt abandoned by someone or many of the choices I made which led to many of those difficult and traumatic outcomes. Today, I am **defined** by one thing only and His name is Jesus and I'm good with that.

Colossians 2:10 TPT - And our own completeness is now found in him. We are filled with God as Christ's fullness overflows within us. He is the Head of every kingdom and authority in the universe!

I seriously just love how Holy Spirit can take normal everyday words and turn them around to bring about a new and improved concept and perspective into discovering and uncovering my holy identity, and how to successfully walk through life securely anchored to it. Until I came out of agreement with everything false, I had believed about myself, my family, church and God, Jesus and Holy Spirit, nothing and I mean nothing was going to ever change. In addition, I had to love myself enough to choose to come out of partnership with the pain of my past. I, in a sense married my pain and the covenant I made with it had to be broken for me to move forward into healing. For such a long time, I gave the pain and whomever I *believed* inflicted me with said pain, incredible power over me by reliving it repeatedly in my thoughts, which affected my actions. Once again, just because I believed they caused me pain does not mean they set out to, or they perceived it as painful. It was my brain and the emotions I allowed to control me that perceived it as pain. As long as I **grounded, rooted, anchored,** believed as **truth, established** in and was **defined** by my brokenness; believing I was a bad person, the world was against me and life was one huge pile of poo, I was going to stay stuck and in many cases smothered and covered in the poo, I myself created. Can I get an Amen! My pain was the **foundation** of who I believed I was, and so created a very rocky and broken structure for me to live on and by, remember the fault line? I was **anchored** to my pain, to my shame, to rejection, the lies and feelings of abandonment, and since I was **anchored** to it, I stayed there. It was in my cocoon time where I discovered this and chose to uproot the anchor firmly placed in the past pain, and then cast anchor into Gods heart and His word so I could move forward and become who I was created to be based solely in His truth, not the worlds and not my past.

Here are just a few areas that can be impacted by faulty and unstable **foundations** along with poor root systems leading to a wounded and broken identity which will always produce wounded and broken outcomes.

- Who we choose as friends?
- Whether we challenge ourselves or not.
- How we see authority.
- How we treat our own bodies and others.
- What level of education we go after and why?
- Who we choose to marry?
- How we choose to treat our spouses, friends, our self.
- How we treat and raise our own children.
- How we see ourselves and others. (What lens we look through)
- How we react or respond to accusations. Do they define us?
- Whether we take offence or not and what are we choosing to take offence to.
- Whether we set goals and go after them or not.
- Do we finish what we started? (Complete tasks)
- Do we have hopes and dreams? (Can we dream)
- What jobs we choose and why? Is this a job you desire or are you pleasing someone else?
- Who we choose to speak life into us?
- How we see God, Jesus and Holy Spirit.
- Are we able to set healthy boundaries?
- Does your Yes mean Yes and your No mean No?
- Do we need to compete with others to feel important?
- Do we compare ourselves to others? Or Do we feel like we never measure up?
- Do we have social anxiety?

I could go on and on because the identity we choose to knowingly or unknowingly *anchor* ourselves to will impact every area of our life and the lives of others we do life with. I believe it is crucial to discover the condition of our individual identity so therefore, if it does not line up with what God says about us, change can come if we choose. Once we choose to change the way we see ourselves and others, our circumstantial outcomes will too change. Once we line up with the spoken truth from God and how He sees us, everything else will follow suit. We need to first line up within our mind, heart and spirit before our circumstances will line up too. Before I knew any of this, I gave way too much power to so many people and circumstances that played out in my life. God was not the one that determined who I was; man was. I had no idea then that I was idolizing man and their perspectives, not God. Everything I listed above I listed because each are areas I myself struggled in due to the identity I chose to partner with from a very young age. I am speaking from a place of understanding the difference between false identities; *grounded* in lies, fear, shame and pain and authentic identity; *grounded* and *established* in what God says and only God. I am living proof of the healing and transformational power of Gods perfect life-giving love.

Titus 3: 3-7 - At one time we too were foolish, disobedient, deceived and enslaved by all kinds of passions and pleasures. We lived in malice and envy, being hated and hating one another. But when the kindness and love of God our Savior appeared, he saved us, not because of righteous things we had done, but because of his mercy. He saved us through the washing of rebirth and renewal by the Holy Spirit, whom he poured out on us generously through Jesus Christ our Savior, so that, having been justified by his grace, we might become heirs having the hope of eternal life.

2 TOXIC MINDSETS

The poisonous side-effects of flowing in and from mindsets of orphan, victim and slave

---

"If you realized how powerful your thoughts are, you would never think a negative thought."

Peace Pilgrim

What are toxic mindsets? To break it down, toxic means *poisonous,* and is related to the word *toxin,* which is a kind of *poison.* It comes from the ancient Greek word *Toxicon,* which means "*poison for arrows.*" Well, that makes total sense to me because I personally see the lies of the enemy as *poisonous arrows* or darts being fired away and the target is none other than God's precious children. Below is a list of synonyms and antonyms for the word toxic and I am including these so you can see the difference between the *<u>deceitful</u> <u>lies</u>* of the enemy, (synonyms) compared to the *<u>truth</u>* from God, (antonyms).

Synonyms: deadly, harmful, lethal, septic, and venomous
Antonyms: harmless, healthy, helpful, kind, and wholesome

Mindset- is the established set of attitudes held by someone.

To sum things up; a toxic mindset is a poisonous and harmful way to view yourself and others. The synopsis is that many of our life's decisions are made from this place of thinking, and how can that possibly result in positive outcomes? Here are a couple of mindsets I unknowingly partnered with from an early age that opened many destructive doors into a world of continual self-sabotage, loneliness, fear, shame and poor self-image. No one, including my parents forced me to believe the toxic lies I believed. It's my brain and what goes on in my brain and what I chose to partner with and give power to. *People don't have that much power unless we give it to them.*

Orphan

An Orphan Mindset takes on the character traits of believing you are unwanted, forgotten, abandoned, rejected, alone and do not belong anywhere or with anyone. You wander through life believing no one loves you or wants you. You might even feel invisible, overlooked, misunderstood or easily dismissed. If these toxic thoughts continue to go unchecked, you will grow up continuing to produce in your present circumstances more rejection to prove to yourself that you are yet alone, abandoned, unwanted and easily forgotten. The key here is to understand that it's something we individually carry and will produce, not the other way around. I cannot express enough the importance of being educated and made aware of the underlying truth and root of your own mindsets and where and why they originated in the first place. Change will not happen for you until you choose to look inward not outward and instead of blaming and shaming others for their behaviors, first take a hard look at what part you are playing and if this is a typical outcome for you in most of your relationships. *Most likely if the same outcome is continuing to happen but with a different person, job, church group, etc., it is something we are carrying not everyone else.*

I personally do not have many memories earlier than 4-years old which is quite common. However, I can remember as a little girl; approximately 5 or 6 already believing I was adopted and that I did not belong to my family of origin, and this I believed even though I was a twin. There were many times I sat either in my bedroom battling these toxic thoughts within my head or alongside our family dog, Taffy and discussed with her why I believed this to be true. She always listened and it is sad to say, the victim mindset I partner with, had me believing she was the only one who would, and who cared. I continued through life never feeling like I fit in or belonged and so would try even harder to be accepted and liked by my peer groups by people pleasing. Instead of being myself, I morphed into what I believed they would like and approve of. I feared being left out or forgotten so agreed to whatever they asked of me so I would be included. As a young child, those agreements personally, did not inflict harm upon me, but as I grew older, agreeing to drugs, drinking and sex, even when I did not want to, did.

I continually felt like I was overlooked, unloved, ignored, a bother, a burden, invisible, unworthy of love and attention and an outcast, no matter where I went to school or what friends I chose to hang out with. I felt alone even though our family consisted of seven. I had this sadness and loneliness feeling inside me all the time that I just couldn't shake, nor did I understand. No matter how hard I tried to feel happy, I couldn't. Even at holiday events, I always felt like I received less than my siblings did, and I can remember so many Christmas mornings waking up, opening presents and then being sad due to the lens I was choosing to look through. I so desired to change this about myself but had no idea what the underlying issue was nor did I have the necessary tools so to uncover the lies I believed about myself and those I lived with. I was stuck in a holding pattern of seeing everything first through a filter of orphan and victim so continued to stay almost paralyzed and unable to move forward with this mindset anchored firmly in place.

One of the first stops Jesus took me on as I pursued complete inner healing was uncovering my thoughts of not belonging and not feeling loved or wanted. He led me to a podcast on orphan mindsets and just like that, it all made sense. Everything the Pastor was preaching on; I could relate to and it brought me such peace finally just knowing someone else struggled like I did and got it. So, I wasn't crazy and there was hope.

As I began passionately and aggressively educating myself in orphan mindsets, I had to dig into my past to find out where it all began; when was this door opened in my life so I could shut it once and for all. As I allowed Jesus's truth, His light to come into the places of darkness within my heart, spirit and soul, my thoughts of not belonging turned into thoughts of knowing who I belonged to and that was God Himself. I made a conscious effort to hold *every* thought that did not produce life within me, captive and get rid of it. I replaced those toxic thoughts with life giving ones straight from His word and His word only. During this mind transformation phase, Holy Spirit showed me a toilet and said, "flush the lies away!" Since then, I have mastered the art of recognizing quickly the root of the thought and I

hit the flush handle the second I know it is not a holy thought but a deadly toxic one. Today, I see my brain as a beautiful creation by God and I am passionate about protecting and loving it by keeping anything harmful at bay.

2 Corinthians 10:5 - We demolish arguments and every pretension that sets itself up against the knowledge of God, and we take captive every thought to make it obedient to Christ.

As I aggressively and faithfully set out on my quest to uncover the root of my orphan mindset, I grabbed ahold of the source I knew would be the best guidance counselor and that would be Jesus. His word says to ask, and you shall receive so I stepped out in faith and did just that. As I asked Jesus to disclose to me where it all originated; He quickly responded by showing me a memory of my mom continually saying to me *"Your dad wanted to stop at two kids, but I wanted more."* Since I was her 3rd pregnancy, what little Marcia Ann heard was "Your dad did not want you." Do I believe my mom said this to intentionally hurt me? Of course not! She had no idea she was producing those thoughts inside my head, that's my brain not hers. I was the one who chose to give those words so much power over me and allowed it to determine what I even thought of myself. She too was a wounded individual with needs unmet herself, and just trying to parent the best way she knew how to. Today I get that and so forgave her when Jesus showed me that memory which is a very important step, but I still needed to allow little Marcia Ann to feel what she felt so she could be free from that pain of rejection and move on. If I chose to continue to hang onto what was causing me brokenness inside, I would continue to create brokenness around me, and I would also continue contaminating my life today and I was just so over that. *Forgiveness is necessary but so is feeling and releasing.*

I am a firm believer in challenging myself so I can achieve breakthrough and freedom and I came up with a little slogan I like to call *The Three C's – Commit to Challenging* yourself to *Change.* I can tell you from personal experience and coming from a place of both orphan and victim mindset, it required me to *accept the challenge to commit to the change necessary within my own being for my circumstances today to change.* I knew it was not going to be easy because it was a belief system and mindset I had partnered with and planted firmly in place for a very long time, but I now knew and accepted that I was worth it and I knew that no matter what, God was not going to leave me, which for someone who believed she was alone was already a huge step in the right direction. In addition, I also came into agreement with His word that says; Greater is He that is in me than he that is in this world so

I knew that God within me would be able to grant me the strength necessary for every challenge I faced.

1 John 4:4 - You, dear children, are from God and have overcome them, because the one who is in you is greater than the one who is in the world.

Victim

A **Victim Mindset** is a type of mindset that seeks to feel persecuted in order to gain attention or avoid self-responsibility. Think about that for a second, **SEEKS to feel persecuted?** Okay, so first and foremost, it's a feeling not a fact. Just because you feel persecuted does not mean you are being persecuted. I for one,

"Victims declare; "The world is responsible for me", and never do anything to better their quality of life."

Dr. Henry Cloud

produced my own persecution within my head and did not need the help of anyone else. I can also say this in love and grace for myself, Thank you Jesus! That I persecuted others when I believed they wronged me and they became my victims, yet I believed the whole time, I was their victim. My mindset, my actions, my outcomes. Hear me when I say this, we are producing what is happening around us and to us. Come on now! If you believe you deserve to be punished in life, you will produce in your current relationships a sense and atmosphere of punishment. You will produce it at work, at home, school, church, small groups, etc., etc.

It's a feeling, a mindset and something you are hanging onto and believing in, it's not everyone else's issue or thought process. This can also involve you punishing others because you believe they have victimized you, when in fact you possibly produced it. You will attract rescuers to you who will continue to enable you to stay a victim and, in a sense, take your power from you by not allowing you to solve things yourself. I don't know about you, but when I accomplish a task on my own, or complete a goal, I feel empowered. It's a great feeling and allows me to believe in myself as someone capable of achieving and accomplishing things and this builds my confidence to set new goals and go after achieving those as well.

Many victims become persecutors of their rescuers like I just shared with you from my own life and cause the rescuers to become their victims. Did you get that? Victims desire to be rescued but resent the ones who rescued them so eventually persecute them. If you are a rescuer, you will attract victims to you so you can rescue them and fill a need within you that was never met. You become empowered by your rescue and unknowingly take from the victim an opportunity for them to be empowered by figuring it out themselves. It's just one messed up triangle of emotional dysfunction. The truth is that the only one who can rescue you and save you from a place of brokenness into a place of pure love and acceptance, not from a place of needing to feel important or powerful, is Jesus.

I'm not finished with victim, sorry; this mentality will also convince you that life is not only beyond your control, but that everyone is deliberately out to get you! This type of toxic thinking results in constant blame, finger pointing and many pity parties that are fueled by pessimism, fear and anger. My question and I might challenge you here, and I hope that is okay; who are we giving power to with this mindset? If we believe people are deliberately out to get us? Do we then believe that we are that powerful to cause other people to possibly sin? Does everyone have nothing better to do than think of ways to get at us?

As a recovering victim, I can honestly say that the only person I thought about was myself. I remember believing that everyone was either looking or talking about me when I entered a place of business, a restaurant, church or store, and I always believed it was negative. What I was not aware of is that I was giving myself a whole lot of power over a whole lot of people by believing that. Like they have nothing better to do but stop dead in their tracks, because I just entered the place? Good grief! The best part of this eye-opening gold nugget of truth was that I realized how much God loved me because He desired me to be healed from what was continuing to hold me back and poison my day to day life. He never sugar coated anything, but then, I did not want Him too. I desired to learn, grow and change so my outcomes could change too. Trust me when I say, with love for myself; I am just not that important, and people have way too many other things going on in their own lives to stop and only focus on me. That was me and me only and my toxic thinking that was leading me to believe those lies. That was the wounded little child within me still needing so badly to be seen and heard and so desperately desiring to be celebrated for who she was; separate from her twin and older sister; just her own unique and beautiful self. The flip side of this is that I was the one doing the judging, whether of my parents, my sisters or people in general, so therefore planting seeds of judgment, and so the fruit of my harvest was judgment, not grace. I was producing what I believed to be true due to the seeds I was planting.

In addition, if you are a believer and have Jesus Christ living within you, then how can you consider yourself a victim when Christ was and will always be victorious? Forgive me if some of my questions and points might sound harsh, but I am here today free of all these toxic mindsets due to these tough questions Holy Spirit asked of me, and the greatest change came once He made me aware of it and no sooner. You will hear me say throughout this book that *Awareness Leads to Wholeness*. When and only when I challenged myself and got real, was I then able to stop hanging out and being buddies with orphan and victim mindset. *I had to choose to change the way I was thinking for my life circumstances to begin to change too.* If you are unsure whether you flow in this mentality or not, look at some ways a victim sees things throughout life, so if you choose to, can begin to step out of these ugly mindsets.

- You're constantly blaming other people or situations for feeling miserable.
- You possess a "life is against me" philosophy.
- You're cynical or pessimistic.
- You see your problems as catastrophes and blow them out of proportion. (You tend to exaggerate your circumstances to receive more attention.)
- You think others are purposely trying to emotionally hurt you.
- You believe you're the only one being targeted for mistreatment.
- You keep reliving past painful memories that made you feel like a victim.
- Even when things go right, you find something to complain about.
- You refuse to consider other perspectives when talking about your problems.
- You feel powerless and unable to cope effectively with a problem or life in general.

- You feel attacked when you're given constructive criticism.
- You believe you're not responsible for what happens in your life (others are).
- You believe that everyone is "better off" than you.
- You seem to enjoy feeling sorry for yourself.
- You attract people like you (who complain, blame, and feel victimized by life).
- You believe that the world is a scary, mostly bad, place.
- You enjoy sharing your tragic stories with other people.
- You have a habit of blaming, attacking, and accusing those you love for how you feel.
- You feel powerless to change your circumstances.
- You expect to gain sympathy from others and when you don't get it, you feel upset.
- You refuse to analyze yourself or improve your life.
- You tend to "one-up" people when it comes to sharing traumatic experiences.
- You're constantly putting yourself down.
- You say things like…. "I'm waiting for the shoe to fall of the other foot. "or "Everything comes in threes."

If by chance after reading this, you realize for the first time that it is possible that you have a victim mindset or mentality; it's okay. There is no shame or finger pointing here, just awareness so you can enter a new gate of wholeness by flushing any future toxic thoughts that coincide with this mindset and begin replacing them with His victorious truth. And don't forget, it is finished so that means the victory is already won.

John 19:28-30TPT - Jesus knew that his mission was accomplished, and to fulfill the Scripture, Jesus said: "I am thirsty." A jar of sour wine was sitting nearby, so they soaked a sponge with it and put it on the stalk of hyssop and raised it to his lips. When he had sipped the sour wine, he said, "It is finished, my bride!" Then he bowed his head and surrendered his spirit to God.

I personally love Psalm 91 and whenever I feel myself entertaining victim thoughts or revisiting any past mindsets, I begin declaring it into my spirit and literally see myself smothered and covered in this scripture like the hash browns at Waffle House.

Psalm 91NIV

Whoever dwells in the shelter of the Most High will rest in the shadow of the Almighty. I will say of the LORD, "He is my refuge and my fortress, my God, in whom I trust." Surely, he will save you from the fowler's snare and from the deadly pestilence. He will cover you with his feathers, and under his wings you will find refuge; his faithfulness will be your shield and rampart. You will not fear the terror of night, nor the arrow that flies by day, nor the pestilence that stalks in the darkness, nor the plague that destroys at midday. A thousand may fall at your side, ten thousand at your right hand, but it will not come near you. You will only observe with your eyes and see the punishment of the wicked. If you say, "The LORD is my refuge," and you make the Most High your dwelling, no harm will overtake you, no disaster will come near your tent. For he will command his angels concerning you to guard you in all your ways; they will lift you up in their hands, so that you will not strike your foot against a stone. You will tread on the lion and the cobra; you will trample the great lion and the serpent. "Because he loves me," says the LORD, "I will rescue him; I will protect him, for he acknowledges my name. He will call on me, and I will answer him; I will be with him in trouble, I will deliver him and honor him. 16 With long life I will satisfy him and show him my salvation."

Slave

The definition of slave is - *A person who is the legal property of another and is forced to obey them.* In biblical days, slaves were chained up and unable to live in freedom or the life  they desired to live. A slave was bought with a price and he served his master until he is freed or dies. Many were born into slavery so in a sense, they never knew of another lifestyle other than the one they were born into. They accepted it as their fate in life and that is where they existed. They came into and exited this world as slaves. Slave like victim mindset, keeps you confined within an imaginary prison cell and far away from your Kingdom identity and calling. You might not see the shackles and chains with your physical eye, but just because you cannot see them does not mean they are not there. And just as the slave born into slavery, remains trapped, believing this to be their destiny and *"the cards they have been dealt."* (victim quote), these toxic mindsets of victim and slave are very similar. They too will entrap you into believing you deserve what is being done to you and in many cases, produce it within your own lives so you can prove yourself right. The difference between the two is that a slave born into slavery had no choice and was trapped and imprisoned where living with a mindset of slavery is a personal choice.

As I continued to hit the replay button with many of the toxic thoughts swirling around within my brain, I allowed these toxic thoughts to have power over me instead of the other way around.

I unknowingly became a slave to these toxic thoughts, imprisoned to and defined by. As I chose to freely flow in and from these false and toxic perspectives of myself and what I believed about love, pain and significance, I drifted further and further away from reality and God's truth. In doing so, I became a slave to many other masters, but the one that dominated most of my thoughts, the one with the loudest voice, was shame.

Throughout my wandering years in the desert, I switched back and forth between masters depending on who I was trying to please most, God or sin. At times I allowed fear to control and paralyze me, and I did as it commanded, other times; lust, jealousy, anger or even vengeance. Whatever I focused on pretty much became my master and my god of choice at that time in my life. I have discovered through this transformation journey that fear was behind the scenes throughout all stages of my life, most likely something I was born into and became accustomed to, almost like if I was not afraid than something was wrong. There's the twist where we can believe that fear or shame is normal and even necessary, so therefore settle and not challenge ourselves to change because of this belief, when in fact, it is not normal at all and both are damaging to our authentic identity.

I know from experience how crippling this mindset can be because I have walked through this tricky and at times very slippery path this mindset produces. Since I did not see myself as God did; there is no way I could have, if I partnered with a slave or victim mindset, I was easily persuaded by the enemy to engage in activities that would only produce further pain. Here's another twist; since I believed pain and love were one in the same, as I experienced pain, I felt loved. Sad but true. And since I view life through a lens of victim and slavery, I believed I deserved this form of love.

As I chose to believe these toxic lies, I continued to produce an atmosphere of slavery and victimization within me and around me and therefore, fueled both mindsets. These mindsets overtime, increased in power due to the amount of attention they received from my thoughts and my spoken words, affirming their existence. The lie with this mindset is that we are not slaves when we can choose to break free. No one forced me to make the choices I did or put some hocus-pocus spell on me to think the way I did. I made the choices to lock myself away behind bars believing this was the life I deserved, and I also had to be the one to choose to step out of the prison cell and claim my kingdom inheritance. I had to be the one to choose victory as a daughter instead of remaining a slave to sin and shame.

Romans 6:6 says: *We know that our old self was crucified with him in order that the body of sin might be brought to nothing, so that we would no longer be enslaved to sin.*

As I discovered the true meaning behind the victory and sacrificial love demonstrated at The Cross, my need to imprison myself in my past broke away because I realized that if I chose to continue to walk throughout life as a slave to my sin, I was *betraying* everything the cross represented. Jesus died for all my sins and transgressions and staying a slave to my sins was like saying every bit of pain, anguish and turmoil He endured was just a waste of time. Once I came into agreement with my kingdom identity is when I discovered the truth about this mindset and just how deadly and deceiving it can be.

Truth: A child of God is Free!

Okay, so how are you doing right now? Take a second and if necessary, take a deep cleansing breath and tell yourself *"It's going to be okay."* And if you don't like me right now, that's okay too. I know it is not always easy to discover things about yourself you might not necessarily want to be made aware of. Just know that in the scope of life, it's just a thang (southern drawl here) and God in you and with you has got it! He's so much bigger than our junk so this too is not anything He can't handle. I for one *LOVE* to discover areas within me that need to be tinkered with so I can get out of agreement with that yukiness, and into agreement with what God says and nothing else. The thang about orphan, victim and slave mindsets is that they go directly against God and how He created us in the first place. God says in His word that He will never leave us as orphans, so we are basically calling God a liar by partnering with any of those mindsets.

1 John 4:18 - There is no fear in love. But perfect love drives out fear, because fear has to do with punishment. The one who fears is not made perfect in love.

God is also a God of His word, will not go back on His promises and is not Co-dependent, so will not change His mind about His handiwork. He does not succumb to peer pressure; His love is steadfast and true. He was well pleased with His creations back then and nothing has changed. He saw it as *Very Good*, not mediocre or so, so. We are the ones that partner with so many lies about ourselves, others and God which stunts our growth in connection with the Father of truth. There is nothing about God that can lie so whenever we believe lies, we are coming out of agreement with The God of *Perfect* Love and into agreement with the one who lies and uses fear, which is the accuser himself.

John 8:44NIV - You belong to your father, the devil, and you want to carry out your father's desires. He was a murderer from the beginning, not holding to the truth, for there is no truth in him. When he lies, he speaks his native language, for he is a liar and the father of lies.

Left behind

During my quest for deep inner transformational healing, God uncovered a truth that even to this day brings me peace which is *He was always pursuing, loving and protecting me even if I was unaware of it.* Just because I was unaware of His presence did not mean He was not present and active in my life. I was unaware of it primarily due to my wounded and tainted perspective; my victim, orphan and slave mindsets at that time believing I was alone, excluded, trapped, unimportant and whatever I did was not good enough. Partnering with these mindsets and perspectives kept me away from seeing truths so there was no way I was going to recognize the hand of God, since He is Truth. As I walked hand in hand with Jesus, uncovering and restoring, I learned early on the importance of submitting to, and partnering with God and so gave Him permission to peel away the layers of junk so He could go deeper. In this healing process, He showed me times in my life where traumatic memories I had never dealt with were continuing to contaminate all my adult relationships. This is when I can with all honesty and certainty say that God loves very well and so desires us to be healed so we can be all that He created us to be. He wanted me out of my junk more than I did because if I was hanging onto the things that held me back, I was not going to be able to move forward into what He desired for me.

As God, Jesus and Holy Spirit joined forces, working together uncovering layers upon layers of toxic debris, purging from within me past lies I believed about myself, others and even God, they uncovered a memory that I would have sooner forgot about but They knew it needed to be addressed so I could know the truth and be set free. This one memory had poisoned so much of my adolescent and adult life and I had no idea I had given it that much power, but God did and so wanted it dealt with once and for all. He desired for me to know the truth so I would stop contaminating my life today based on the lies I believed from this one memory. I don't believe this was the door opening of my victim mindset but I do believe it was my victim and orphan mindset that not only produced it but kept me living my life stuck in the trauma of the memory instead of dealing with it and moving forward. *STAYING STUCK GIVES POWER TO THE SUBTANCE YOU ARE STUCK IN,* which in my case was the trauma and the feelings this trauma produced.

The first time I was made aware that boys aren't always very nice, can be trusted and might not have your best interest in mind was a night my twin and I decided to go to a different high school dance

48

of a friend of hers. We were having a great time and since I am an extrovert, enjoyed dancing and meeting new people. I was very naive and innocent at the age of 15 and had only attempted to kiss a couple of guys to prove to my peers that I was a normal teenage girl. I had no idea what sex was other than what I read in the very small pamphlet I was handed at health class in school, and I pretty much just looked at the pictures and believed what my mom had taught me which was nothing other than it was dirty and something you did only when married. This new group of friends I had made decided to leave the dance and go on a walk and so I agreed to join them along with my twin and her friend.

We were in an area of town I was not familiar with and the walk took us into the woods. We stopped at an area with a fire pit and some homemade benches where we proceeded to sit down and talk. One of the boys approached me and sat down next to me, leaned over and whispered in my ear: "Are you here with any of the other guys?" I smiled and hesitantly shook my head no, not sure of what he was getting at, but liked the attention. He then asked me if I wanted to go for a walk and I said sure! In my mind, we were just going on a walk and there is no harm in that, so I thought. I had no reason to believe otherwise. We started walking and even though it was at night and we were in some woods, I didn't feel scared or worried; I knew my twin was close by and that always made me feel safe. To me and from my perspective we were two people walking at night in the woods. He however had a different perspective and plan and had not clued me in. He stopped walking, pulled me to him and started kissing me. I tried to pull away and stop him, but he was too strong and forceful with his hands and mouth. I had my lips closed tight and continued to try to get away. I was in shock to say the least and I had no idea a teenage boy could or would be like this. The next thing I knew, he pinned me to the ground, and I could hardly move or breathe. He was a big guy and weighed much more than my 98 pounds. I kept trying to get him off me but could not move at all beneath his weight. I continued to fight, keeping my lips tight and squirming beneath him the best I could. I could not scream or even talk due to the pressure of his lips to mine, in addition to the weight of his body on my chest. Panic gripped me and to this day when I feel confined or heaviness on my chest, whether a tight seat belt or tight hug, I feel the anxiety rise within me, our body remembers.

He began trying to unbutton my blue jeans with one of his hands but was having difficulty; Thank God for tight, Levi's button-down jeans! There were 5 buttons and no zippers! I guess between me squirming and his inability to unbutton my jeans, he became frustrated, got up abruptly and took off! I, however, was left lying there on the pine straw and leaf mixture, and for the first time felt the rain hitting my face and the dampness of the ground beneath me. In the craziness of the moment, I had not even been aware that it had begun raining. I sat up in shock and disbelief of what just happened. No one had ever prepared me for something like this. Fear quickly set in, along with confusion. I picked myself up, brushed myself off and quickly assessed my situation. As reality set in so did many other emotions. My first thoughts were; where am I? And what the heck just happened? I became overwhelmed with fear, confusion, shock, some thankfulness but overall totally shaken up. It was pitch black and I could hardly see my hand in front of my face which only added to my fear and confusion.

I was standing in some very dark and now very scary woods; ALONE! I do remember praying for God to help me find my way back to the fire pit and my twin sister where I would be safe again. I started walking in the direction I believed we had come from. I sensed correctly and exited the woods where the group had been gathered in a circle talking. Once again fear gripped me along with shock... they were all gone! All I could think about at that moment was my twin had left me! How could she? I now began crying because in addition to the first trauma I had just experienced, I was now dealing or trying to deal with a second one. From my 15-year-old perspective things looked very tragic and gloomy. It was dark, raining, my twin left me, and I was lost; enough said! I had to do yet another quick assessment of my situation which concluded that; I was still in the middle of the woods, it was very dark, there was no moon light due to the cloud cover, and I had no earthly idea which direction the school was. I had not been paying much attention when we had walked into the woods since I instead had been talking and following the kids in front of me. All I could remember was that at some point along the way we passed a large pond.

Thank goodness, the rain had stopped so that was a help and I prayed to God again and started walking in the direction I believed was right. I came upon the pond and a bit of hope sparked up in me. I was going in the right direction! I soon found my way back to the school and once inside, found my twin. I was wet from rain and tears, still confused, hurt and angry now too. "How could you leave me?" were the first words out of my mouth when I found her enjoying herself inside the gym. She reassured me that she only left because she had assumed that I had walked back to the school with that guy. That made total sense to me and so the thought of her abandoning me subsided but that was about it. Since down deep I believed it was my fault and I had made a bad decision, I kept what happened a secret believing the lie that if I told my parents, they would punish me for leaving the school in the first place and possibly my sister too. There was no one I considered safe enough to talk to about this, so I didn't.

Orphan, victim and slave mindsets individually are corrupt, however together wreak havoc on your day to day life choices and perspectives which will inevitably produce spiritual and visible, outcomes that will take on the look of a wanderer, a gypsy going from place to place, job to job, relationship to relationship, never ever reaching your promised land, your God ordained purpose and calling, These mindsets convince you that you have no voice, and in many cases that might be very true since you will produce what you believe is true. That night I shook my head "no" because I did not want to hurt his feelings and I said "yes" to him because I did not want to hurt his feelings and agreed to take a walk when deep inside I honestly did not want to. So basically, I made my decisions not on what was best for me or what I really wanted, but what I believed would please and be best for him. That my friend is Co-Dependency at its finest! I placed his needs above mine. I couldn't say no because there was a hidden need within me to be noticed, chosen and to belong that far outweighed the need to say no. One of the lies I believed was that if I said no, he would not like me and possibly get mad at me. Who cares? I can say that now as a healed, 56-year-old but then, I seriously believed that and couldn't bare offending him or possibly hurting his feelings. Like I had that much power?

Since I kept these feelings of failure, shame, abandonment and fear inside by not speaking about my traumatic experience, they were able to stay inside and have their way within me. It was not until this healing journey that I have been walking on and at times running, that I was even made aware of how much emotional pain my 15-year-old self had endured that night and had chosen to hang onto. As Holy Spirit placed this memory upon my heart, I knew the time had come to go back and help my 15-year-old deal with and heal from this tragic experience.

As Jesus led my adult-self back into the memory, I discovered that my 15-year old self was still stuck in the middle of the woods, drenched with rain and tears. I had left her; terrified, alone, ashamed, lost and feeling abandoned. I slowly walked up to her and sat down next to her and introduced myself and Jesus. Since I had already taken this approach with my 7-1/2-year-old, she knew who I was and was already willing to trust me. I thought to myself, how cool that was, not knowing exactly what to expect. I asked her if I could hug her and she said yes. I sat in the middle of those dark and wet woods rocking my teenage-self back and forth in my arms, whispering sweet words of comfort, validation and empathy.

I apologized to her for leaving her in those woods that night and asked for her forgiveness; promising that I was here for her and would not leave her again. I then asked if she had anything, she needed to get off her chest. I listened to her heart regarding the matter she found herself in that night and I validated her feelings of confusion, abandonment and the questioning of her own decision-making skills. Jesus stepped in and explained to her just how much He loved her, she was not alone, and that He was there with her that night even though she did not see Him. I then asked if she was ready to say goodbye to the pain, she took on that night from her attacker, and any lies she partnered with. I explained that she did not need to own his pain or the memory of that night anymore if she chose, and when she was ready, could hand it all over to Jesus and we could get out of these dark woods once and for all. She agreed, forgave her attacker and released all the pain she had owned into the welcoming arms of Jesus, stood up, grabbed mine and Jesus's hands and at that split second, the entire scene changed and the three of us were no longer standing in the middle of the dark woods, we were now standing in the middle of a beautiful meadow with lush green grass, colorful flowers, a beautiful blue sky filled with birds and wispy clouds and this giant oak tree stood off in the distance. The three of us began to run in the direction of the Oak Tree and I knew at that exact moment within my adult-self that the transformation had taken place within me and my 15-year old was at peace.

If there was a time machine and I was able to physically go back and speak to my infant, toddler, preschool, school age and teenager self, I would tell her how amazing, beautiful, perfect, brave, lovely, courageous, funny, creative, intelligent, talented and unique she is regardless of what anyone else says or thinks, but because it is how God made her to be. I would also introduce her to just how much God loves her and does not disapprove of her because she might have sinned. I would introduce her to the welcoming arms of Jesus and explain that He loves her no matter what she receives on a test, what she looks like or whether she pleases her parents or not. He just loves her because that is who He is. I would encourage her to be all she could be and to not let *fear of failure* get in her way. I would tell her that she is capable of whatever she sets her mind to, to believe in herself and her abilities, to celebrate the person she is, all of her. And finally, to not need to receive her worth from any guy or even from her parents, siblings or friends, but just from God.

So many of my decisions I have made throughout life, I made because I needed to feel loved, accepted, seen, heard and be of value to someone. I needed to matter and feel like someone chose me, when I had been seen, heard, valued, accepted, unconditionally loved and chosen all along by God. The little girl within me was still crying out even though she was in the body of an adolescent, young adult and adult. The little girl who believed she was a failure, feared man and the possibility of letting others down, abandoned, dumb, dirty and never knew that "no" was an okay answer, continued to make decisions that pleased everyone else instead of pleasing herself or God. She became a people pleaser instead of doing what was best for her. She grew up unknowingly placing everyone on a pedestal; herself included, instead of the only one who deserved that pedestal position and that was God.

Exodus 20: 3-5NIV - "You shall have no other gods before me. "You shall not make for yourself an image in the form of anything in heaven above or on the earth beneath or in the waters below. You shall not bow down to them or worship them; for I, the LORD your God, am a jealous God, punishing the children for the sin of the parents to the third and fourth generation of those who hate me,

Let me reassure and encourage you that it's okay to take care of you and see to it that the people that are speaking into you produce life not death. It is also important to take care of you by forgiving those that you believe have hurt you and that may even include forgiving yourself because even giving away your power is a form of betrayal and neglect towards yourself that you are choosing to do. I can honestly say that when I chose to say Yes instead of No in the woods that night, the teenage boy did not have a gun to my head or have me in a headlock. There is a very good chance that he would have accepted my No, but I will never know because I chose to not practice at that time owning my own power and instead chose to hand it over to him. In addition, I took from him the opportunity for growth and maturation in character that he might have learned if I would have declined his request for a walk. *Change happens when we look inwards not always outward.*

I realized after going after my 15-year old self that the one who abandoned and betrayed me the most was me. I had no idea at that time in my life, but I was betraying myself by becoming a people pleaser, instead of being true to my own needs, wants and desires. I betrayed myself every time I change my mind to please the other person or morphed into someone to their liking, in hopes of being accepted, loved or approved of. Every time I said yes and meant no; betrayal. Every time I said no when I wanted to say yes; betrayal. This gold nugget I discovered once again while digging deep inside my cocoon transforming my inner pain into joy.

3 *MY BROKEN GLASS SLIPPER*

Yes, mindsets do matter because they foreshadow many of our life's choices and therefore circumstances. In no way am I making an excuse for the choices I made or the toxic behavior I chose by placing all the blame on my toxic thinking. Yes, I partnered with those toxic mindsets, but that does not excuse my behavior with the next story I am going to share with you. When push comes to shove, I knew the difference between right and wrong and still chose wrong. My point here is to educate and make you aware of the importance of what you are allowing your brain to be consumed with. We choose what is going to occupy up space in our beautiful brain. It is important to see negative thoughts as toxic and harmful to improve the future you. Many of my life choices were a result of the toxic beliefs I anchored myself in and therefore began living from. *The thing about anchors is they keep you in one place instead of allowing you to move forward.*

I also want to make something else very clear regarding all my stories throughout this book; they are from my perspective not anyone else's. That's the thing about personal stories; it does not mean it is exactly how things played out to everyone else involved. I am almost 100% positive that if I asked my twin to relay to you her perspective of that night at the dance, she would have a completely different story to tell because it is from her point of view not mine, and possibly even the guy who in my eyes assaulted me. Each of us individually is created differently and with different mindsets and experiences in life therefore we are going to look at life and events from different lenses, and that is okay. To tell someone they should not see something a certain way is basically taking a posture of control and power over them. We are trying to control their brain and their own perspective, when that is not ours to own or control.

Regarding the story you are about to read, I am not going to make any excuses for my behavior or choices I made. I am a firm believer of owning my junk and not blaming others, nor will I own theirs. If I were to make excuses, then I do not truly own anything.

It was now the summer of 79 and I quickly stuffed away the events of that night in the woods and reset my focus on what truly mattered to my now 16 year old self and that was to find her Prince so my life would be complete and I would finally achieve inner happiness. My prayers escalated to a whole new level requesting of God to hurry up and bring him to me, the sooner the better! He answered my prayer that July while I was at Six Flags with a friend. We kept winding up in the same line at different rides and eventually began talking and soon riding rides together. He lived about 30 minutes from me and went to a different high school, but he met all the important criteria's; he was Catholic and super cute.

I fell madly in love with him by the 5th date and believed this was not only my Prince but the man I would one day ride off with into the marriage sunset.

We both were new to this whole relationship thing so took everything slowly and it wasn't until about 5 months in that he told me he loved me, and my life was now perfect and complete. We continued dating on weekends and experiencing life together as boyfriend and girlfriend including backseat make out sessions which were the best. I loved being his girlfriend and was crazy about him. I looked forward to talking to him every night and seeing him on weekends. I put my all into it which meant all my other relationships suffered; girlfriends, myself, family and God, and I slowly placed my Prince on a pedestal, worshipped him and our relationship and left my own identity in the dust. So basically, the one terrified of being abandoned; abandoned her friends, her own hobbies and activities and God too. Hmmmmm???

We both desired to stay pure but slowly the backseat make-out sessions intensified and about 2 years into the relationship, hesitantly made the decision to no longer remain virgins. Due to the heavy amounts of guilt and shame we experienced that night and the nights that followed since now we couldn't seem to stop, our relationship took a hit and about 6 months later; after attending mass together he decided it was a good time to end things in the church parking lot. The moment the words left his mouth, I went into hysteria. I could not believe what I was hearing and was not prepared in the least for. In my eyes and from my perspective everything was fine, and we were continuing to do life together the best we knew how to, and I was so completely happy with that. If he was in my life and choosing me, things were great. He explained all the reasons behind his decision to make himself feel better;

college soon, my parents think its best, but I heard nothing, nor did I understand. All I heard was "I don't want you anymore!" "I am not choosing you!" "I don't love you!" "I had sex with you and now am leaving you."

I was completely confused, in shock and devastated to say the least. One minute he was telling me he loved me and making love to me, and the next ending it? I sat in the driver seat of my car and wept for what seemed like eternity. The feeling of having no say in the matter, my feelings and thoughts were not considered, and I must accept his decision regardless of how I felt. My choice or voice did not matter, well that seems familiar. What I wanted in this relationship did not matter.

The feeling of rejection was something I had never experienced at this kind of level. Yes, I had been rejected in the past and Yes, I had felt unimportant at times even within my own family unit, but this level of rejection was beyond anything I had ever known possible. It was like my heart had been taken out of my chest, smashed into a million pieces and then stuffed back in. I found myself yet again; alone, abandoned, with no voice and no one there to comfort or console me. My car now was taking on the look of the Elementary school hallway and the woods.

To say it broke my heart is an understatement and since in my dreams this kind of thing never happened, I was not prepared and just like the night in the dark woods, had no idea how to handle something like this. My entire identity had been placed within this relationship, the love from this boy and its outcome and this outcome was not exactly what I had believed was going to happen. I had placed so much importance in this young man, our relationship status and our happy ending and now that it came to a screeching halt, the way I saw it, my life was over.

Since I had not been living my life for me but for this relationship, I had not even considered any alternative plans for my future so when it abruptly ended so did all my hopes and dreams. My value, worth and yes, identity was in this boy and what I believed our life together would look like. My whole life from the moment we met when I was 16 revolved around him, our perfect life together not God and not myself. I had already in my dreams selected the wedding dress, our home and how many kids; their sexes, names, how they looked, you get the point. Since I believed deep down, I was a bad person and deserved to be punished, it was very easy for me to now believe I deserved this and once again my victim and orphan mindsest decided to come out and play. This one relationship experience unfortunately became the lens that I then chose to look at all relationships through and to say that I had walls up is an understatement. I began telling myself to not trust love and stay on guard and protect your heart because you don't know when a surprise attack will occur.

Whether history loves to repeat itself or maybe because I am reproducing it, I did not believe I had anyone safe to go to and had no idea how to process through my pain, so I didn't. I did what I knew to do and so stuffed it away with all my other traumatic experiences, but this time my heart turned hard, cold and off. I went into isolation, consumed myself with my pain, made friends with it and continued to nurture my already established victim and orphan mindsets. I unknowingly sunk into deep depression and pretty much gave up on caring what happened to me now. I did not matter so neither did any of my desires. My prayers now consisted of pleading with God to bring him back.

This would have been a great time to have close girlfriends, but I had been so engrossed in this relationship for 2-1/2 years that I had put all my close friendships on hold so to dedicate 100% to my Prince and our future together. My unexpressed and not dealt with pain began calling the shots and I started on a long journey of self-punishment due to all the shame and self-hate I chose to come into agreement with.

What little advice I remember receiving from my mom to console me was along the lines of "There are plenty of fish in the sea so the best way to forget about a guy is to get another." Today my adult self understands that my mom honestly had no idea how to console her daughters aching heart. This was an area she never experienced herself so therefore she really could not empathize with me. Unfortunately, for me and from my wounded perspective, I did just that and gave myself no time to mourn, grieve the loss and eventually heal. Regardless of what her advice happened to be, I still was the one that chose to follow that advice instead of listening to my own heart and do what was best for me. I pleased her not myself.

Within a month I had met another guy who I immediately slept with because down deep, I really didn't care—in my eyes and from my own perspective, my dreams were shattered and I just wanted to be loved and be chosen again, Pick me! Pick me! My mom was right, the excitement of this new relationship was like a drug and it did help me forget about my Prince by silencing some of the pain. I quickly hit the "repeat" button and like with my Prince, I placed all my identity and worth in this new guy. It's like I just transferred my identity like I would money in a bank account. He too dumped me as well after first telling me he loved me and in a very nasty way and this rejection so soon after the first one resulted in my physical body hemorrhaging. I did not even know that was possible, but it is. I remember waking up one night feeling as if I had wet the bed but instead my sheets were covered in blood. My heart was broken, and my body was bleeding. The doctor said that my body was responding to my emotional pain and so was preventing me from getting pregnant. I was an emotional and now physical mess. I continued my shame cycle of going from one guy to the next in hopes of drowning out the pain inside me of betrayal, rejection and the loss of my hopes and dreams. At this point, I didn't care if they loved me or not because I sure didn't love myself and love was just a 4-letter mean and nasty word!

My twin, who by now was accustomed to trying to talk me off the ledge, suggested we go to Florida to visit our Grandma for the 4th of July to get away and I believe she was just trying to help. To this day, I have no idea how we survived that weekend other than the grace of God. On our quick trip to Florida I had met a young man at a club and before the weekend was over, had slept with him. I do not remember much of that encounter due to the amount of alcohol and drugs I had taken in. I basically just remember waking up once and became aware that he was on top of me having sex with me. Lucky for me, Florida guy happened to live in Georgia and since I had zero respect for myself, whenever He "needed" something, I obliged and since I still had no voice, even saying "No" to his advances didn't really mean "No." To be completely honest, by this point, I really didn't care anymore. In my wounded 18-year old's mind, I had screwed up big time and my forever dreams and the life I thought I was going to live out was already over so I was going to need to accept the scraps thrown my way.

I continued my lifestyle choice of seeking out new relationships and the excitement from the lure and first sexual encounter throughout the summer and fall months. I unknowingly was on a journey of self-destruction and punishment and in just a short six month period of time, I had been raped twice, had multiple attempted rapes and I have no idea how many men I had chosen to sleep with out of a sense of duty, not desire. Since I had placed all my identity, my worth, my value and my significance in my Prince and our happily ever after, I never once considered my own hopes, my own dreams, my own purpose on this planet, my talents or gifting's, so therefore never thought about life after Prince. The only hope I had was that one day my Prince would return and then my life would be complete again and until that happens, what's the point? Sad but true.

Thanksgiving was about three weeks away and I finally had something to be grateful for. God must have been listening after all because my Prince decided to call and wanted to see me over his holiday break. I quickly went from an attitude of life is over to there is hope again and all because I received a phone call and was asked on a date. It's like my life had been on hold and now with that one call the start button was pushed again. I quickly resumed my dreaming of a future now that my Prince was returning, and this small gesture brought bounce back into my step and my life now had value and purpose. In my young 18-year old mind, the man I already imagined marrying was coming back and this must mean that he truly loves me and is choosing me. I had been living by the quote, "If you love something, let it go, if it returns, it's yours; if it doesn't, it never was." This one simple phone call ignited a ray of hope at a time that I felt very hopeless and very discouraged. It is sad for me today to think that I thought so little of myself and my own life, my purpose and value that I allowed a guy to determine it all for me.

Around that same time, I was informed by my twin that Florida fling and his brother were planning to visit a couple of weeks prior to Thanksgiving and SHOCKER, during the time our parents would be "out of town." Since I had recently heard from my beloved Prince, I wanted nothing to do with that arrangement and had thought I communicated that. The last thing I wanted was to mess anything up with my Prince by hanging out with Florida fling. I had no desire or need to see him anymore since now my life was back on track. Unfortunately, and not with my approval, Florida fling came over with his brother and expected to receive from me what I normally gave him. The nerve of him! This time, I did not want to oblige but he didn't seem to understand the word No! I finally gave in and just let him do what he needed to do and what he had been used to. About 5 minutes later, (maybe less) it was over, and I was outraged! I'm not sure who I hated more, myself or him. Why didn't I fight more? I became so angry that I kicked him out of my room and insisted that he go and sleep in his car, which I believe he did, and I really didn't care. That was the first time I expressed anger at a guy for going against my wishes instead of just displaying anger towards myself. I did what I normally did and quickly stuffed and pushed the thoughts of that night behind me and placed it back on my Prince returning soon and all the excitement around us possibly getting back together.

I honestly have very little memory of my Prince and our date other than it ended with fear sex which consisted of me believing that if I did not have sex then he would not need me anymore and throw me away again. Whether we continued to stay in contact other than that one date, I do not remember. I believe my brain still is protecting me from some of those painful memories at that time in my life and that's okay.

Fast forward 4 weeks; Christmas was around the corner and I had left work early due to some recent stomach issues and found myself in our family doctor's office. I was a closet smoker at the time and even that I could no longer stomach. My family doctor originally diagnosed me with a nervous stomach but before prescribing any meds, asked me if there was any chance, I could be pregnant. When he asked the question, I was completely thrown off guard. The question he asked me was, "Have you been sexually active?" I remember feeling like he could see all my shame, guilt and disgrace written all over my face so in a panic and since he knew my parents, I quickly responded with NO!! He must have sensed my knee-jerk reaction and sweetly changed his wording a bit, so it sounded less offensive for me. I then felt safe and responded with yes and to make myself feel better and less dirty, I lied, saying it was with my boyfriend of almost 3 years. Somehow to me, that minimized my sin and the guilt and shame I was carrying around.

I did as the doctor asked and gave him a urine sample and waited very nervously for the results. When he came back into the room, I could sense his sadness as he looked at me and said the test results are positive. I remember at first not quite understanding what he meant by that since I had never taken a test before. Did positive mean yes or no? You are positively not pregnant? Well, he once again changed his wording and cleared everything up for me when he said, "You are pregnant."

It's as if the words left his mouth and smack me upside the head, they were such a shock! My entire future seemed to have flashed before my eyes in a split second and the fear that rose up inside me was overwhelming to say the least. Until that day and at that moment I had no idea fear, shame and guilt could be that suffocating. He was so kind and asked if I would like him to speak to my parents and I quickly said "No!" I might be in complete shock but one thing I did know was that it might not be too smart to let the parents in on this just yet. I was sobbing at this point and saying to myself, "This can't be true!" "It's just a nightmare and you will wake up soon." "Tests have been wrong before." I somehow managed to drive home in total shock and through heavy and at times uncontrollable sobbing. Let me back up a few months here…. When I had started hemorrhaging several months earlier the doctor had prescribed for me birth control to stop the bleeding and get my cycle back on track. Apparently, I missed a day and since I had not been taking them for too long, I was highly fertile. The thought of being pregnant had never crossed my mind! I honestly had never thought I could be pregnant, even with the stomach issues. I truly believed at 18 that pregnancy only happens when you are married plus in addition, I was on birth control.

Growing up the topic of sex was not something we discussed in our household but what I did know about it was that 1. It was not discussed. 2. It was considered dirty since certain parts of my body were. 3. It was not discussed. 4. It was only for a husband and wife. 5. It was not discussed. And finally, 6. If you had sex before marriage, you would burn in hell. In addition, this kind of stuff never happened in any of the fairytales I read nor in any of my dreams.

Everything was going south in a hand basket and I went from having some hope to hopeless with one blink of an eye. I had no idea how to even begin processing through any of this. I had been living this secret life my parents knew nothing about and I had been lying to everyone around me including myself. Who was I anymore? Oh wait! How can I possibly know who I am when my whole purpose and value is based on whether a guy loves me or *not?! I did not know or recognize this person I had become, and I so did not like her, I loathed her at this point. I had not only betrayed others, I had betrayed myself not only by placing all my importance in a guy or what others think about me, but also by devaluing and dishonoring my body by having sex with multiple partners. I was now pregnant at 18 and had to figure out what in the world I was going to do with this baby growing inside me. Let's not forget, God and I had a one-sided relationship which consisted of me reaching out to Him when I needed something and that's about it. There was no way I could face Him knowing the lifestyle I had been choosing to live and now to boot, I was pregnant out of wedlock and not sure who the father was! I knew I not only had sex but sex with three different guys over a period of about 5 weeks. During my months of self-hatred and self-punishment I had never stopped long enough to think about the consequences of my actions and now I was forced to face a big one head on.*

As I drove home from the doctor's office, my brain was bombarded with thoughts coming from all sorts of different directions and all at once. What am I to do? Who is the father? Why me? How do I tell my parents? Do I tell my parents, or do I get an abortion? If I get an abortion, where do I get the money to pay for it? Can I even get an abortion because then I would burn in hell for sure! What am I to do? What am I to do? WHAT AM I TO DO?????? The more I thought about it all, the more I cried. Before I made it home, I was able to rule out the guy from where I worked because I remembered getting my period around Halloween which was after that sexual encounter. Oh, good grief! My life was looking more like a soap opera and I was the crazy main character with all these secrets hoping no one will discover what they are.

I knew that I was going to soon be home and face to face with my mom and I had to get my act together and fast. I was never very good at lying straight to my mom's face and she always seemed to know when I did. At this point, I was already going to burn in hell for having sex outside of marriage so what's one more lie? As I pulled into my driveway, I was relieved to see my mom's car was not there. I quickly made my way into the house and into my bedroom where I tried my best to get myself put back together. My makeup was smeared all over my face from all the crying so I washed and freshened up, but the tears just kept coming so my lie would have to involve crying due to sickness. No matter how hard I tried to make the bad thoughts stop, I couldn't. I kept hearing over and over in my head…. "This can't be really happening!" It's a nightmare and I am going to wake up soon." "What are you going to do?" "You are going to be such a disappointment to your family." "Look at the mess you have gotten yourself into!" "You have totally screwed everything up now!" Those inner thoughts continued to play repeatedly in my head like a broken record.

I practiced in my bedroom mirror what I was going to say to my mom when she returned home as if I was rehearsing lines for a movie script and in a sense, I had been living out a lie so I was getting pretty good at acting. I heard my mom pull into the driveway and I panicked. I knew that she was going to wonder why I was at home since I should be at work. I quickly did a once over and prepared myself for her questioning.

Sure enough, a few minutes later there was a knock at my door and my mom asked what I was doing home. I quickly responded with what I had rehearsed; I had left work early due to my stomach issues and had seen our family doctor, he's so nice! I then explained that he said it was just a nervous stomach and to go home and get some rest. It wasn't so difficult to lie with a door closed between us. I lay back down on my bed and quietly cried and berated myself so she would not hear me.

It wasn't long before my mom came back to check on me. How do they know certain things? This time, she wanted to see me, so I opened the door and stepped into the hallway. We had floor to ceiling mirror tiles on a wall at the end of the hallway which gave the illusion that the hallway was very long, 80's decor at its finest! The two of us stood in front of the mirrors and I had a very difficult time looking her in the face, shame kind of does that to you. I played off the tears by saying my stomach really hurt, and it truly did. The next words that came out of her mouth sent shock waves up and down my spine. She said, and I quote, "Marcia Ann, are you pregnant?" My inner voice in my head was saying.... "What the_____ and how the _____ did she know?!!" I hesitated for just a second and with my best straight forward answer said "What?" and "No!" Like, really? How could you even think that of me???

Unfortunately, my tear ducks had not been in on the discussion with my brain earlier and decided to strike and continued to leak an annoying watery substance from them, and just like that I couldn't contain it any longer. What is it with mothers and their ability to stir up certain emotions within you? I surrendered to all the emotions, whether hormonal or teenmonal and began sobbing and just started shaking my head, yes. The next thing that happened impacted my life even until this very day. My very traditional, Catholic and strict Sicilian mother took me into her arms and hugged me and began rocking me back and forth. My first thoughts were who is this woman? Where is the UFO ship that landed and abducted my real mother? This was not the mom I had grown up with for 18 years, but I really like this one and this hug feels good. Through the tears, I heard her ask… "What are you going to do?"

I still had those terrible annoying thoughts racing through my mind but having my mom show me this much grace was something I had never experienced before. This was the very last thing that I imagined happening. I thought for sure that the minute I had told my mom, I would have been sent to a home for unwed mothers so none of the neighbors or church folk would know.

My mom stopped hugging me and now had my hands in hers. She looked me in the eyes and said that she loved me and that she would support me in whatever decision I would make. Okay, that's it! Where is she? Who is this imposter?!!! I remember the exact response I had that day standing hand in hand with my mom in front of those glass tiles. I said, "I don't know why, but I already love it." We stood there, I cried quietly, and I knew that she knew exactly what I meant. A special bond was birthed at that precise moment that to this day I treasure and hold very dear my heart. The way she chose to respond that day allowed me to witness a side of my mom I had never known or seen before. I believe for the first time, I met Jesus within her. It opened a place in my heart of love, admiration and respect for this woman standing before me that to this day I still carry. To the young adolescent literally feeling like her world was crashing down upon her, it made a huge impact. It meant so much to me to know that I had her support and it gave me just a glimmer of hope, security and safety at a time I needed it the most. I knew that breaking the news to my dad would be very difficult but knowing that I had the support of my mom helped ease some of the fear and nervousness building up inside of me.

Since I had always placed so much importance in what my parents thought of me, this upcoming conversation with my dad was a hard thing for me to deal with on an emotional level. I could deal with the physical changes already happening within my body, but it was the emotional ones I was challenged by. Let's face it, hormones are already all over the place during pregnancy and add what I was dealing with to the equation? It was a lot for my young 18-year-old self especially since how I dealt with trauma before was to stuff, not cope. I knew deep down inside that very soon I was going to have to speak out loud and in person the words that had been swirling around in my brain to my dad and I did not want to hurt his heart this way. I had desired so badly to be approved of and accepted by him and I knew that what I was about to share with him would most definitely affect that and what little connection I already had with him.

As I lay my head down on my pillow that night, I watched as the events of the day played out in my head like a movie reel. I was still in shock and denial of all that had transpired within this one day. When I had awakened just this very morning, life was quite different. The only worry I had was to get ready and head to work, possibly see the doctor about my stomach and that's about it. Now I lay here just a mere 14 hours later, consumed with fear and thoughts of my future. I had mixed emotions between the discovery of my pregnancy, an overwhelming fear of my future, sadness and shame-knowing my predicament of not knowing who the father was, but in all that mental wrestling, there was a hint of hope due to my mom's loving and grace-filled response. I knew this was a big decision I had to make that would impact my life forever but to have my mom's support was huge and gave me some breathing room and made me feel like it was going to be okay. To be perfectly honest, I wanted so badly to have it all just go away. I wanted to pinch myself, wake up and see that it was all just a bad dream.

Unfortunately, I woke up the next morning and nothing had changed. I was still pregnant and somehow put myself together enough to head to work and pretend that I nothing was wrong. Previously during our sweet time in front of the glass tiles, my mom and I discussed and agreed on telling my dad the next evening. I dreaded this with every ounce of my existence but knew it had to be done. No one is ever mentally prepared for something like this, so I seriously struggled all day at work with the thoughts of the night to come. I had always feared my dad and I feared everything about the conversation I was about to have with him. I had never given my dad a glimpse of that side of me, so I knew he was in for a shock.

I was home from work, dinner had been eaten, dishes cleared and cleaned and the dreaded time had come for me to spill the beans to my dad and at that moment I believe I would have preferred to have been sitting in the dentist office having my teeth pulled and without Novocain. Instead, I took my mom's lead and found myself sitting across from my dad who sat on the couch and even though my mom was there for support and encouragement, I was overcome with fear and shame. Our family room was a good size but that night it felt very small and I desperately wanted to escape my reality like I use to do with my Barbies. How does one even begin to tell her dad that she is pregnant? There is nothing in my life that prepared me for this moment, Nothing! I stared at this man, my hero in a sense and hated what I was going to have to say to him. The little girl still wishing she could jump in his lap knew deep down that after tonight, things would change, and I would be lucky to ever be accepted again. Would he still love me after I tell him what a disappointment I am? I hated every part of this person

I had become. I sat there struggling to just get the words out; they just did not want to come. I finally got enough nerve up to just say them... Rip it off like a band aid! "Dad, I'm pregnant!"

I remember to this day the look of shock and disbelief on my dad's face when I told him. My mom had wanted me to tell him, she was there only for moral support and I know that was the right thing to do. I had been adult enough to sleep with someone and become pregnant, so I was adult enough to face my dad and explain my adult situation I got myself into. I experienced at that moment an avalanche of sorrow, pain, remorse, regret, disgrace, disappointment, fear, failure, and unworthiness, just to name a few. His look alone generated that within me. He could have spoken nothing, and I still would have known what a disappointment I was. Something I never ever wanted to hear or sense from my dad but that night I got a double portion of both.

His look of disapproval, disappointment and disgust did a number on me and I immediately knew how I just changed what little relationship, if any, I had with him. My dad sat there and at first, I believe he thought I was joking around. He looked at my mom in disbelief and then at me. He even asked... "Is this a joke?" No, dad it`s not! It's not April 1st! Oh, how I wish it was. Can I be like Dream of Jeannie and snap my fingers and all this will go away? Oh, how I wish I could. As my dad's brain began processing through what he just heard, the questions began coming like rapid fire. How do you know? Are you sure? What are you going to do? How did this happen? Who`s the father? What were you thinking? I don't think I heard any of the questions except "Who is the father?" Not that question! That one I have not processed through completely yet, so this is not a good time to ask.

He repeated himself again and due to all my shame and need to keep things safe for me, I convinced myself that I couldn't tell them the truth about my pregnancy dilemma. I couldn't tell them about Florida fling and him being at our house while they were out of town at a time like this. They had only met him once and had no idea I was still seeing him. I did not want to jeopardize the grace I was experiencing with my mom and I knew if I answered my dad's question honestly, the you know what would hit the fan for sure. My brain quickly began processing through how terrible a reaction I would receive if I came clean. As I sat there in front of my parents; a ware was raging within my brain and soul. Do I tell them the truth and suffer additional consequences? Or Do I play it safe and tell them what I believe they are ready to hear? I do have fifty-fifty chance of this baby being Prince's and those are pretty good odds.

And as my dad repeated the question a 3rd time; "Who is the father?" I chose to play things safe and responded...... "It's (Prince's child!")

I was raised to not lie and had to go to confession every month to confess my sins, yet here I sat telling the lie of all lies. How did I get here? Once again, I began questioning who I had become. How could I just lie about something like that? My inside voice was screaming this at me and then there was the other voice convincing me that this was the safest path to take, the path of less backlash, the path that's easier for me. I was listening to the wrong voices and had been for some time now so why would this be any different? The reason I was in this predicament to begin with was because of my previous choices. I had decided to not say anything about it and cause my dad any additional pain, but the truth is; I didn't want to cause myself anymore pain. Yes, I was afraid of my dad, Yes, I was afraid of failing him and disappointing him, Yes, I was afraid of letting him down but all those put together does not justify me lying about the dilemma of not knowing who the father is. I can go on and on with excuse after excuse as to why I did what I did but when all things are said and done, the bottom line is that I acted out of selfishness and pride and did what was easier for me and only me. Yes, my dad's initial reaction might have involved anger and a few choice words but in the long run, telling the truth is always best way to go for all involved and I wound up learning that the hard way.

The dreaded conversation was over, but this time I did not feel the warm fuzzy's I had felt after my time with my mom. Tonight, I felt so ashamed of what I had just done in addition to dealing with the fact that I knew that he was so disappointed in me. I did however, experience a sigh of relief that both my parents now knew, not the complete truth but the fact that I was with child and my fear of being kicked out was not going to play out like I had originally thought.

My bargaining and negotiating prayers now changed to pleading and begging God for this baby to be my Prince's not Florida flings. I took on the position of a Circus Ringleader hoping He would jump through my hoops and perform for me. I made my bed God but I'm asking you to give me a whole new bed to lie in with new sheets, a dust ruffle, pillow shams and bed spread to boot. I don't want this one anymore. There was a part of me that believed that God wouldn't do this to me and allow me to become pregnant from a man who forced himself on me. Nah, He's not that kind of God. How quickly the enemy tries to get us thinking badly about God, so we wind up blaming Him instead of looking at ourselves.

I was being eaten up with the lie I was telling along with the biggest decision of my young life; do I keep it or give it up for adoption? This was a huge decision my 18-year-old self needed to make and to be honest, emotionally I was not in a good place. I realized that this was a baby growing inside me that I would now be responsible for a very long time and that part alone was overwhelmingly scary. It was not a hamster or a goldfish; it was a baby that would be relying on me for his or her existence for the rest of their life. I was not prepared at all to even know how to deal with this type of decision of this magnitude. I was truly hoping now, with my parents informed, that I could just resume with my life; working full time and trying my best to deal with my pregnancy, the decision I needed to make and the future of this baby growing inside me. I was not expecting my dad to do what he did next.

My dad being retired military, believed in boundaries, rules, consequences, fairness and doing what is right. I on the other hand was well practiced in the art of sweeping things under the rug and just deal with my situation alone. I get the image of Steve Martin in the movie 'The Jerk'. There's the scene after he loses all his money and he is going around the house with his pants down around his ankles saying...... "All I need is this lamp and that's all I need." Just like Steve Martins character in The Jerk, I too was trying to cover up my inner pain by saying that I was fine doing things on my own when in all honesty, I was not. Since I had not been completely honest with my parents about Florida fling and since my dad believed in doing what was right, they decided that the next step was for me to inform Prince and his family. My dad believed that since this was Prince's child growing inside me, he needed to be a man and help raise it. Okay, wait a minute! Cut! Take two! Dad, that is not in the original script playing out in my head! You cannot just come in here and start moving things around and make my life more difficult. That is not fair to me and my lie! Come on now! Get with my program!

When I did enter into times of rational thinking, I would tell myself that the simplest thing to do would be to come clean and tell them about my dilemma but on the flip side, there was that annoying voice that kept telling me that they would hate me forever, so don't.

To be obedient to my parent's request, I reluctantly dialed Prince's number to inform him that I was pregnant. Prince's mom answered and I said Hi! And asked to speak to her son. When he came to the phone and I heard his voice; the raging battle within my mind I experienced the night before with my parents started up again and I struggled with getting my words out for a couple of reasons; one- I found it hard to speak out what I believe will not please the other person, being a people pleaser and two – I knew the whole truth and was about to lie to my Prince. I finally broke the silence and managed to inform Prince of my situation the best I could and like I predicted, things drastically changed.

I remember as if it was yesterday, the silence on the other end followed by him saying…. "I need to get off the phone because my mom is standing at my bedroom door and must have heard what you said." She apparently had stayed on the line to talk to me so had heard my announcement to her son without us being aware of her presence. I quickly sank deeper into my pit of shame and guilt and this place was becoming quite comfortable for me. I felt terrible when I got off the phone and for my young 18-year old self found herself again having no idea how to process through the inner turmoil going on within me, so I did what I was comfortable with and didn't.

So, the cat was out of the bag and at that point I no longer had a voice and it did not matter what I wanted anymore. Both sets of parents took it from there and for starters a meeting was set up later that week for us all to get together and discuss what steps to take next. This virus I created was growing and spreading quickly and more people were being affected by my lie, but I still refused to come clean. Daily, I berated myself and listened to all the negative voices telling me what a terrible person I was. I had several new and negative tenants moving into my mind and I was choosing to allow them to stay free of rent. The only thing that kept me going was the love I was already feeling for this unborn child growing inside me. I had numbed myself in so many other areas but there was this one feeling that crept up on occasion—my hope of love and at this moment it was toward the baby developing inside me.

My life was changing in all areas and at times it was very overwhelming and scary. I still had not decided whether I was going to keep the baby or not and so having these feelings towards it at such an early stage of my pregnancy made me realize how much I loved it and that maybe I could be a good mom. This sweet feeling, I was experiencing is what eventually led me to the decision to keep it.

The night had come to meet with Princes' parents and discuss my predicament. The parents congregated together in the family room and discussed my future and what they believed was best for me while Prince and I hung out in his bedroom. I rested in his arms and for a moment, I felt safe and home. I began daydreaming about us being married and raising our baby together. I shared this with him and there was no response. He had been going to college about 4 hours away and his mom and dad had other plans for his life which was the reason behind the break-up with me 7 months earlier. I loved him so much and wanted nothing more than to one day be his wife and have his babies. It would be my fairytale ending come true. Oh, how I wished it could have been that easy.

Well, that is not at all what happened. That night was the last time, I allowed myself to dream and believe in fairy tales and happy endings. My glass slipper fell off and my Prince Charming did not pick it up and run after me. He did not choose me, no one did. I left that night feeling very broken, sad and alone among other things. As my parents and I drove home that night and once again from my perspective, my life as I saw it was rocky, unstable and out of control and in many ways it was. Nothing appeared familiar or safe anymore and this brought about immense feelings of insecurity and a sense of isolation. It's like trying to get your footing on slippery, pointy rocks while wearing stiletto's, which is not going to happen.

The plan the parents decided for me was to wait until I went for my first OB-GYN appointment, find out the due date and we would take it from there. My victim-self believed I no longer had a say which was a lie because I did but chose not to come clean so instead went along with their plan of action. I was consumed with shame and guilt, knowing deep down that I had just ruined both my relationship with my Prince and his parents regardless of the outcome, things had drastically changed. I suffered that day a loss that I wasn't ready to deal with or knew how to process through, so once again, I didn't.

I was scheduled to see my OBGYN and my mom came with me. I sat in the waiting room and believed everyone was staring at me knowing that I was unmarried and pregnant out of wedlock even though I was barely showing. I felt like Hester Prynne in the Scarlet

Letter but instead of having to wear a red letter 'A' on my shirt, mine was a 'W' for wedlock or better yet, Whore. I just felt ashamed all the time and almost became paranoid that people were whispering about me behind my back. All I could think about was what a disgrace I was to my family, my Prince and his family too. I eventually made it back to see my doctor and was quite surprised when I was able to hear my baby's heartbeat for the first time. I was not expecting that so for a moment, I felt excited about something. He had a heartbeat! The doctor believed that I was about 6 weeks along and I was given an estimated delivery date as well. This made things scarier because now there was a set date of the arrival of this baby that I had no idea how to take care of. Next in line was to inform Prince's parents the outcome from today's doctor visit.

I'm not sure what all was said because my dad had phoned Princes parents in his bedroom, but there was a heated discussion going on and I could tell by my dad's tone that he was not happy. My parents got off the phone and made their way into the family room where I was seated and let me know that Prince's parents said that there was no way this baby was his because the due date did not match up. I was not sure what they were talking about because all this pregnancy lingo was new to me. It was not long ago that I believed you had to be married to get pregnant so I had no idea how someone could determine whether the baby was theirs or not based on a due date. What was familiar to me was the feeling of rejection and not being chosen again. That was something I was quite aware of and understood. I feel incredibly guilty and ashamed of myself knowing I did this but in addition the amount of rejection I was dealing with completely consumed me and in a sense, I relived that moment in the school and in the car all over again.

Once again, I was ready to put everything behind me, pick up the pieces and move forward knowing what my secret was, but dang it if my dad did not see or feel the same way. Before I could blink an eye, he hired a high-standing lawyer and the weight of shame and guilt increased 10-fold. To ease some of my inner turmoil I decided to face the music and shared with my mom the possibilities that my baby could not be Princes. She once again surprised me with her response by not shaming me but reassuring me that everything was going to be okay. My secret now became our secret and things stayed the same with the lawyer and the lawsuit against my Prince. My life literally was placed on hold until a paternity test would be taken once my baby turned 6 months old.

I continued through life the best I could, each day experiencing a new symptom in pregnancy whether with emotions, fatigue or nausea. I was working full-time so was able to get insurance with the company and they came on board, supporting and helping me. (God moment un-noticed) I went to my monthly doctor appointments and purchased the right books to start reading about what to expect when I am pregnant. I had an amazing friend of my mom's step in and start investing time in me, praying over me and teaching me about nursing and natural childbirth by taking me to both Lamaze and LA Leche League meetings. In addition to her, I had a Sister-N-Law that was a total gem. She never once shamed me but instead loved and supported me. She invested so much time in me whether shopping for nursery items, maternity clothes or baby necessities. She became a safe place for me and the 2nd person I eventually told my secret to.

The days and months passed by quickly and the time was here for my baby to be born. I wound up being about 11 days late and was so ready to meet him or her. I remember my dad calling his place of business and telling them that it was Labor Day even though it was the middle of August and that made me laugh. He was also telling me that if I didn't hurry up, he was going to carry me himself to the car. Thankfully, we all arrived at the hospital with my contractions being about 5 minutes apart and about 4 hours later my beautiful son entered the world naturally weighing in at 8lbs 41/2 ounces. Bless his little heart; he was not happy about leaving the cozy world he had lived in for 9 months and in many ways, neither was I. Reality quickly set in as the doctor handed him to me and I was now holding this little baby boy in my arms and I had no idea what to do next. The nurses began cleaning the two of us up and the emptiness I felt when leaving Prince's house that night washed over me again. I was alone, rejected, not chosen. Nothing had changed in my emotional world, so I continued to view things from a victim and orphan mindset. The only changes that had occurred were that I was now 19 years old and holding my baby boy in my arms. In addition, the reality of this baby being completely dependent upon me was extremely overwhelming. It was not a dream; it was the real thing. I was a single mom and I had a baby boy that was dependent on me for his life and I could not even take care of myself so how in the world was I going to take care of him? No psychologist or self-help book could have prepared me for what I was experiencing at that very moment.

After my time in recovery, one of the nurses in charge of me began to push me out into the hospital hallway to take me to my room and that is when I saw my son in his own incubator being pushed out as well. I remember this as if it was just yesterday, well my heart and spirit do because it meant that much to my 19-year-old self. My dad happened to be standing nearby and he walked up and stopped my gurney. He went over first to get a peek at my son, his first grandson and then he came back over to me. He leaned down, *kissed my forehead and said... "Thank you for my grandson, he`s perfect. I love you." That memory even though it was over 37 years ago still blesses me and brings sweet tears to my eyes. I tried at the time to hold it together but as the nurse began rolling me to my room and further away from him, I couldn't fight back the tears and so I cried.*

That young 19-year-old had been longing to hear those words from her dad her whole life. That day in the hospital hallway I experienced something new; my dad told me he loved me even though I had let him down, had caused him pain, had disappointed and in many ways hurt him.   Those words were more than just music to my ears; they were music to my heart, spirit and soul. I know those tears that were shed that day were not just from sadness, loneliness or fear but tears that came from the little girl in me so needing to hear and feel loved, accepted and to be chosen by her dad regardless of her actions. Those three sweet words pierced and briefly awakened a part of my heart and spirit that was lying dormant—dying and aching to be loved, chosen by her dad and to matter. I believe I cried from both the 19-year-old and the little girls' wounded and broken heart as well. It goes to show you how much power is in our tongue and our actions.

As I chose to partner with all my toxic mindsets, I became blinded to the truth happening around me that proved otherwise. Toxic mindsets, whether shame, victim, orphan or slave keep us out of agreement with the word of God. They produce in our life the opposite of what the promises and blessings that God bestowed upon His chosen, from the beginning of time. Since I had partnered with those mindsets, I was unaware of the hand of God working so beautifully in my life. God showed up so many times; whether at my place of employment, a mutual friend of my moms, my sister-n-law, my mom's grace, church or the beautiful words of my dad spoken over me at the hospital. All those moments were God moments, yet I was completely blinded to that truth due to the toxic lies I believed. I can say with 100% certainty that the part of me that agreed and partnered with unworthiness, orphan, shame and victim quickly discounted those beautiful words my dad spoke to me.

At that time, I was consumed with fear, guilt and shame and *what consumed me, shaped me.* From my 19-year old perspective, filtered through my toxic mindsets; I was very much alone - (orphan) and would have to figure everything out myself - (victim) and everything I did in life was bad - (shame). That's the thing with shame and the other toxic mindsets of orphan, victim and slave, they keep you from receiving spiritual and physical blessings because you convince yourself that you do not deserve or are worthy of anything good, and everything God creates and produces is good so unknowingly you resist the blessings God so desperately wants to bestow upon you. God's promises are *Yes* and *Amen* and a victim will believe; NOT FOR ME, JUST EVERYONE ELSE! An orphan; HE WILL FORGET ABOUT ME and a slave; I DO NOT DESERVE IT SO I NEED TO WORK HARDER. Oh, how I gave so much power to those mindsets.

2 Corinthians 1:20NIV - For all the promises of God in Him are Yes, and in Him Amen, to the glory of God through us.

Everything that I knew and believed about love and dreaming of love became too painful, so I unknowingly shut those down too. Since most of my heart wounds came unexpectedly and without warning, I grew up fearing intimacy and connection in every relationship I entered and so as a means of protection, guarded my heart and kept myself emotionally separated. I became more of a spectator standing on the outside looking in and making those jeering remarks instead of being a part of the team, supportive and eager to learn, grow and win. I entered into every relationship from a victim and orphan stand point; still needing to be rescued and at the same time feeling alone and unworthy of their love so made sure to keep them at arm's length to prove my point that I was unlovable and bad. I then shifted into resentment and retaliation towards my rescuer because it wasn't even what I truly wanted or desired, so the home turned into a warzone. I had no idea that fear was behind much of my outbursts because deep down beneath the layers of prideful protection was a fear to love because I believed they would eventually leave me which would hurt me. The anger was a result of all my fear and pain I stuffed down and never dealt with. I continued to produce failed relationships due to my own toxic mindsets and beliefs. I also attracted to me people who too were wounded; disconnected emotionally and feared intimacy themselves. My twin who is now a licensed Psychologist would always tell me: "You will attract at the level of your healing," and today as I reflect back, I can see how that continued to play out in my life.

In addition, the little wounded girl within me believed that protecting herself from being hurt meant placing all her dreams of love and belonging in a prison cell, shutting the cell door and locking it shut, but she also locked all her emotions in that cell along with herself. I did to her exactly what I believed everyone else did to her. I did not choose her either. My fear of feeling rejected and cast out again trembled deep within me and called all the shots without me even being aware of it. I had no idea of this at the time nor would I have understood it either, but I was the one producing the rejection, abandonment and chaos in all my relationships, not necessarily them. I was the common denominator and I was the one believing what I believed about myself, love, intimacy, belonging and connection. Until I realized and accepted those truths, nothing was going to change, and I would continue contaminating my life today with my judgments of myself, love and men; and my toxic mindsets securely locked in place.

What Consumes you; Shapes you

Please hear and receive this... Whatever you partner with or allow yourself to be consumed by, will shape and lead you. It can even become our gods and something we cling to and worship. Be very mindful of your thoughts and what you are choosing to lead your life choices. If you choose to partner with thoughts of fear, fear will lead you. If you partner with thoughts of lust, anger, hate, rejection, comparison or jealousy, guess what will lead you? Your thoughts are not to be taken lightly. If they are not bringing you joy, peace, hope and love, if they are not thoughts God would have of you or others, then choose to love you by not allowing them to take up space in that beautiful brain of yours.

Thoughts, whether good or bad produce feelings within us which then in many cases lead to actions and these actions lead to outcomes which when broken down are the result of the original thought. If I desired to, I could dissect a situation I am in today and uncover the original thought that produced it. God created these very powerful and beautiful brains of ours and even though they are crazy powerful, He created us with the ability to have control and power over them. God gave you the ability to choose what you want to keep in your brain and what you want to dispose of. He is not a controlling God and gives us free will and that includes our thinking.

It is very important to be aware of just how slimy the enemy is because once you are aware of his schemes and deceitful methods; you can then counterattack with the truth, God's word. Whenever I see kudzu, I think of the lies of the accuser. Kudzu starts out as a small, prickly vine shooting out of the ground and can be stopped at that point with weed killer. If left unchecked though, can and will take over acres and acres of land. Eventually trees, even houses can be engulfed with it and at that point, you must burn it to kill it and sometimes that doesn't even work. This is how I see the accuser when he whispers lies to us. It starts out very small, think of the size of a seed here, has maybe 10% truth to it, but if left unattended, can grow and grow and eventually take over our heart, perspectives, choices, and life. The accuser is not satisfied until he destroys Gods children and if that means having them take their own lives then he has won. The bible says it very clearly in *John 10:10* that the enemy is here to kill, steal and destroy us so it is crucial that we do as Jesus did and fend him off with the truth and power in the word of God. The power is in the name and blood of Jesus and is necessary for the battle raging within us and around us.

John 10:10NIV - The thief comes only to steal and kill and destroy; I have come that they may have life and have it to the full.

What we believe does and will affect our bodies, choices and outcomes. Everything we decide to do in life starts first in the brain. Since I believed I could not achieve a higher education due to my earlier school trauma at 7-1/2 and because I once overheard a teacher say to my mom that I was lazy, I turned down an amazing opportunity to go into a fashion school to become a fashion merchandizer. You already read earlier in chapter 1 how much I loved playing fashion with all my Barbie dolls, but since I believed the lies; that I was dumb, incapable and feared branching out on my own due to not believing in myself and my gifting's, I did not even try. To make matters worse, I quit the job I loved 2 weeks after they offered that to me. I sabotaged the one thing going on in my life I could call just mine, something I loved and was talented at. I chose to believe and be led by a lie spoken to me by someone most likely wounded herself. I gave this one teacher and the words she spoke so much power and importance. My identity was warped because it was anchored to and fueled by words spoken out that were not even true. I was choosing to be led by my fear of failure and the lie I anchored myself to that I was terrible at school, and lazy so don't bother trying. Those were lies I believed and a mentality I allowed to take power over me since I was 7-1/2 and at 18, I was still allowing it to lead me in life. I not only gave the lie power over me but the teacher too.

Your beautiful and powerful brain is like a computer and was created by God to keep files of memories and these files are there forever, whether you want them to be or not. So many times, we try to forget, and we hide them somewhere but just like files on computers, they are always there waiting to be pulled up and used again. I'm hoping this is making you think like it did me and use your brain for something constructive and as a means of healthy mindful change.

Our thoughts dictate so many of our choices in life whether good or bad, so we need to hold ourselves accountable for those thoughts we are allowing to hold up space in our brain. Take care of you and your thinking and the outcomes in your life and the fruit of your harvest will be different. Be good to you and *nurture* yourself well and this includes your brain. Be aware of the schemes of the enemy and know who fights on your behalf.

Let's go a little deeper by discussing the word *Nurture.* The definition of Nurture is; *(to care for and encourage the growth or development of).* I'm going to break it down for you here. People aren't the only ones we can nurture. We can also nurture our emotions or the emotions and behavior of others. What we nurture or give attention to is what becomes more prominent within us. What you learn to nurture will become how you will also cope or not cope with things that arise in your life. You will not only perceive things from this place, but you will also respond as well. This becomes part of your identity. It becomes how you handle or don't handle people and situations in your life. *You will produce in your present life what you believe to be true.* I cannot say that enough.

Another teaching He partnered with nurturing was practicing. He used the saying... "Practice makes perfect." He was referring to my behavior. If I had fallen into a pattern of taking offence and then reacting, I was perfecting that emotional response. I was perfectly practicing this and perfecting it without giving it a second thought. He also explained to me – that if I was taking offence, it was because my heart was easily offended. Once again, first taking a hard look at myself instead of pointing my finger at others. So, ask yourself these two questions... *What have I practiced to the point of perfecting? From what lens or filter am I looking at things from?*

- Love or fear?
- Forgiveness or unforgiveness?
- Grace or judgement?
- Connection or distance?
- Control or trust?
- Rejection or acceptance?

- Peace or War?
- Pride or Humility?

So, are you ready to go a bit deeper? Be kind to you and take a deep breath. When you inhale; receive His grace and when you exhale, release any negative thoughts or emotions. Take time to think about this in your own life not someone else's and ask Holy Spirit if there is an area that you need to investigate, work through, and heal from. There is a reason why we do what we do and for things to change around us we first need to make some changes within. I know I have said that a dozen times and I might say it a dozen more because of how valuable that one nugget of truth is to achieve permanent inner transformational healing. There is always a root cause, or a buried seed and Holy Spirit knows where those roots and seeds lie and wants to remove them. He desires us all to be completely free, not partially and this takes time and commitment.

I realize that all the above questions are not always easy to answer and require us to look back into our childhood and take notice and responsibility for things we might not want to look at or take responsibility for. Sometimes it's not so pretty and can bring up things we don't necessarily want to remember. Believe me, I know, have been in the arena, fought the fight, have the battle wounds and because of God's perfect love, grace and healing power, am on the other side. I want to encourage you here as Jesus has encouraged me through my own inner transformation journey.

- God is with you and is not going anywhere.
- He is way bigger than whatever you are dealing with or are faced with and can handle it.
- He will not give up on you because
- He believes in you.

- He is for you and not against you so is rooting you on through this process.

- He will and I promise, help guide you through to victory.

As you take time to go deeper into your own inner healing, know that you have all of heaven cheering you on and that's quite an army of healing experts and Masters of Ministry. Trust in His healing process and the One who heals. Celebrate this time because one day as you begin looking back, like I do, your first thought will be one of gratitude; knowing that you were loved so well by your Creator and that He loved you through your healing, regardless of your sin. You will call it all joy because of what you have become due to the pain you once had. Your pain will no longer define you, only His love. Your testimony will be one of victory, not defeat.

2 Corinthians 12:9 - And He said to me, "My grace is sufficient for you, for my strength is made perfect in weakness." Therefore, most gladly I will rather boast in my infirmities, that the power of Christ may rest upon me.

4 RINSE AND REPEAT

"Choosing to Change; Changes your Choosing."

I have discovered while on my own journey for inner wholeness that I did not change until I *chose to change.* If I continued to choose what I was choosing, my outcomes were going to remain the same and so they did. If I continued to choose to believe what I believed, my outcomes were going to be the same. A famous quote of Albert Einstein's was *"Insanity is doing the same thing over and over again but expecting a different result."* Yep! That was me blaming everyone else for my outcomes when I was the one making the choices which produced the outcomes.

Studies show that most people do not change in a 5-year period of time. They might change their place of residence, job, hair color, relationship status or weight, but as far as emotionally changing so that their perspectives, choices, mindsets and circumstances change is not as likely. True change, defined as *the act or fact of changing; fact of being changed,* and is noticeable to those we do life with, requires so much more. It requires our behaviors, habits and attitudes to change and that means consistent adjustments within a person's mindset and outlook on themselves not so much everyone around them. It requires at times intentional and intensive self-evaluation, self-reflection and self-awareness which is not always fun but necessary for positive and permanent change to come.

New habits and mindset adjustments do not take only 21 days to form, that is false. Studies show that it takes 63-66 days for old pathways to die and new pathways to be established within our brain, which means constant awareness of our reactions, outlooks, choices, perspective and underlying behavior patterns and thought processes. Why we do what we do; say what we say; react or respond; take offense or not; turn the cheek or fight back; own other feelings or just our own, believe what we believe about God, ourselves and others. Everything is stored up in our brain and produces our life choices and outcomes based on those life choices. If we want things to look different in our life, then we need to look closely at ourselves and why we think the way we think.

This level of change required me swallowing my pride, my stubbornness, my need for justice, to be heard, pitied, always right and instead took a hard and very necessary look at me and what I was doing and why I was doing it, instead of pointing my fingers at everyone else. I discovered this in my own life by accident, although now that I am aware of just how God works, I realize it was no accident at all, but instead His way of preparing me for His plans, yet to come.

My typical relationship cycle went as follows:

1. Praying to God and looking in desperation for my prince, my soul mate.

2. Due to impatience and a lack of value and worth; I

accepted whatever came my way because someone paid interest in me.

3. Placing all my needs, interests and personal dreams aside, God included so to give 100% to new guy.

4. Became whatever they needed me to become instead of being myself.

5. Quickly fell hard and then due to fear, hung on for dear life by being a clingy, needy vine.

6. Living in a state of fear so worrying and questioning the whole time whether they really loved me or not and displaying this with outbursts of anger if they did not do what I expected they should do; which would be to put me first, choose me. (Fear and need to control due to fear.)

7. Pleading with God to show me if they were the one because I just don't want to get hurt again, but terrified to know the truth believing I might not find someone else.

8. The minute I felt anything shift, I quickly panicked, hung on tighter and began needing God again to make things right. My prayers turned to pleas, asking God to show them I'm the one and we are meant to be together. (Treating God more like a puppet not The Creator of All).

9. Once rejected; I would go into self-pity mode with a side of guilt and pursue God again with repentance, rededication and promises to never do it again. Anger would come next with more promises to never trust a man again either and self-abuse in the form of harsh belittling and shaming. *"How could you!" "When will you ever learn!"*

"You are such an idiot!" Etc.

10. In many cases, especially when the guy had manners and treated me with respect, I would not be able to handle that so would sabotage the relationship before I believed he would eventually come to his senses and dump me. (Down deep I believed I was bad, and they deserved better).

11. Rinse and Repeat.

I never once thought about having healthy boundaries or what that even looked like; his character traits, (stable, balanced, loyal, honest, God-fearing, etc.), moral beliefs or whether he was right for me, but instead that I was just so lucky and fortunate that someone actually picked me and desired to be with me, considering my tainted past. My self-esteem and self-worth were non-existent; I had zero dignity, value or respect for myself nor knew how that even looked and let's be honest here, if I did not value or respect myself, there was no way I was going to value or respect anyone else because you can't give what you don't have, period!

This was a cycle I nurtured and perfected from 1979 all the way to 2012. Each cycle picked up speed and strength to move onto the next. I like to describe it to be like a snowball effect which Wikipedia says is *a process that starts from an initial state of small significance and builds upon itself, becoming larger (graver, more serious), and perhaps potentially dangerous or disastrous.* There were extended periods of time between cycles but only due to 2 of my marriages; one lasting 5 years and one lasting 7. This does not mean that I did not manifest certain cycle patterns while in the marriage. I was a slave to fear, shame, regret, anger, orphan and victim regardless of my relationship status. These mindsets and identity robbers caused me to remain unhappy and non-content no matter how nice my spouse was. While I was married, it was always their fault and I continued to believe the same lies I believed before I was married. The mindsets were mine, not theirs. Just because I became married did not mean they went away or the wounds that lay dormant within me would not arise and want justice when triggered within the marriage.

The part of the cycle I was on this one night was immediately following a breakup and it was a doozey, although as a victim, all my break-ups were doozey's. I was trying very hard to busy myself by cleaning out my nightstand table and happened upon a good 10 years' worth of journals which I chose to flip through and read. What I discovered that night I describe as a single breadcrumb placed on the path which eventually would lead me to my own well encounter with Jesus some 7 years later. It would take many more breadcrumbs before I would finally recognize the ultimate truth which is; there is only one Prince for me, and His name is Jesus.

It was September of 2005; I was licking my wounds after my 3rd marriage ended just after only 2 months. I felt like such a failure, a complete idiot and a downright pathetic loser, what's new? Back in July of that same year, I had been on a popular dating site and had been communicating with a guy, and after about a couple of weeks of email and phone exchange, we met in person. Our first date was amazing and before the sun rose the next day, I had sealed the deal with sex. Since this part of the exchange went very well, I became blinded to all truth and reality, fell hard, spent all my waking hours with him, moved my daughter and I before the week was out and was married to him after just a month. Even though I had many people trying to talk sense into me, I blocked them all out. I even remember sending an email to my family using the quote, "Opinions are like buttholes, (keeping it clean here) everyone's got one." Not a very proud moment of mine. I did what I normally did in relationships; I became what he wanted; (sexually too), said what he needed to hear, morphed into what He needed, put God on the back burner, started loving his interests and hobbies, put my passions and dreams aside, clung on for dear life and imagined the perfect wedding and life together. As the day drew closer for our wedding, I had many 2nd thoughts but quickly pushed them aside thinking it was just nervous jitter and I was too afraid to hurt him so continued with the plans. On the day of our wedding I remember my dad approaching me in the bedroom I was getting ready in and he asked me why I was in such a hurry and what would be the harm in waiting? He said if it's love, it will be here a year from now too. I could sense his concern and so reassured him that I knew what I was doing and that we were so in love. The ceremony was beautiful, and we had decided to postpone our Honeymoon until September when the kids were on fall break.

Fast forward to September and the awaited honeymoon, I could tell something was very wrong and he wanted to leave early because he missed his kids. On the drive home, I just knew deep down that he was having 2nd thoughts, but there was a part of me hoping for the best mainly to save face. When we arrived back home, I just asked him straight out "Do you still love me?" and he said "No." I felt yet again, like I was my 18-year-old self in my car in the church parking lot when my Prince broke up with me. It did not matter what I had to say, how I felt or what I wanted, it was a done deal. I quickly became that same wounded victim pleading to know why and what happened? I began begging for him to reconsider and to give me another chance just like I did at 18 with my Prince. I knew the whole-time deep down that he was right and that I did not love him either, but my pride would not allow me to admit to that. It was more comfortable to play the victim so that is what I did. My pride, orphan and victim mindsets quickly kicked into overdrive reminding me once again that I was rejected, not wanted, unlovable, alone and not chosen.

Thank goodness the basement apartment I had previously been living in and had not even moved any of my furnishings from, had still not been rented. I made one quick call just to let my Landlord know I was retuning and was moved back in within the hour. No sooner had I gotten back into my apartment, I phoned my dad and through hysteria informed him of what had just transpired and what a stupid idiot I was. I believe this was the first time I ever screamed and cried that hard to my dad as an adult and I remember him doing his best to calm me down and reassure me that what I was saying was not true and that everything was going be okay. I was in a state of shock almost feeling like I was living out a nightmare and hoping once again that I would wake up and realize it was just a dream. I did the next thing I knew to do to cope and got in contact with a dear friend, went to his house and had pity sex. I did what I knew worked and what might ease some of the heartache I was experiencing. It sure as heck did not help with the guilt or shame, but then that too was something I was accustom to and part of my shame train I was riding on.

I quickly began the detaching phase of the cycle by what I would like to call my bury and scurry move. This common and comfortable move involved me ignoring my feelings (feared them) by burying them deep inside and believing instead that I had dealt with them and that I am going to be okay. The next thing that came very naturally for my victim self was to erect a thicker and more durable wall around my heart so I could keep myself protected from any additional pain. (Fear and anger) The next phase consisted of me internally hitting a "RESET" button so to move on unscathed, so I thought, and determined to not let any guy have power over me again. (Pride). And the cycle ended with me going full speed ahead into seeking God; by going back to church, praying, worship music, time alone with Him in prayer, and journaling all my feelings to Him. This always seemed to ease some of the initial pain. I then made all sorts of 'vows against' and 'promises that I won't,' verbally and in writing. This entire unhealthy process of detaching quickly from husband #3 and reattaching to God took at the most, 2 weeks.

What I was completely unaware of is that burying all that pain and not allowing myself time to process through it, just produced more anger within me and the pride walls of protection kept out anything good as well and that included inner healing. Outside I looked like I had it all together, but internally, I was fuming inside, filled with fear, anger, resentment, bitterness, guilt, shame and self-condemnation and my pride made sure to keep it that way.

What I discovered that night in my bedroom as I combed through one journal after another was the ugly truth that I was living proof of Albert Einstein's famous quote. My cycles seemed to result in the same outcome. I'm going to list it out, so you can see for yourself my patterns/cycles.

1. Shock of an unexpected break-up.
2. Wishing it was just a bad dream.
3. Overwhelmed by feelings of failure, inadequacy, hopelessness, rejection, abandonment and shame.
4. Needing God again and in a sense using Him as another guy to help to forget the former. (ouch!)
5. Making all sorts of promises to not do it again.

The bottom line here; I was the main character in each of my journal entries; different guys, jobs, ink color, residences, but one thing was the same and that was ME. Nothing had changed and not because God hadn't changed or the guys I picked hadn't changed; nothing had changed because I had not! I was just cycling around my mountain of desperation for love, acceptance, value and purpose wrapped up in a man. I read page after page of me either crying out to God about some guy, desperately wanting him to love me, pleading for God to show me if this guy was the one, or crying out to God asking Him to take away the pain I was going through due to being rejected.

The thing about pride and shame is that they blame everyone else and I have found that if you want things to be different in your life, than you are going to need to take a hard look at yourself first instead of everyone else. I was still toting around my bag of wounds and those wounds were calling all the shots. I was still unknowingly planting the same ole seeds of judgement, rejection, abandonment, shame, victim and loneliness repeatedly and so I was still reaping them. This was my mindset, my beliefs, my fears,

"It is necessary to deal and be real with your pain for the truth to be revealed, so you can be healed."

M.A. Congdon

my seeds, my choices, my cycles and until I started looking at me and why I was doing what I was doing; get to the root and begin doing the work necessary to achieve healing, nothing and I mean nothing was going to circumstantially change. My way of processing pain by burying and scurrying is great for critters when storing up food for the winter but for humans; it just keeps you locked away in your pain; believing the lie that you are moving forward but in truth, the hidden pain will keep you stuck in the past unable to move forward into true freedom. *It is necessary to deal and be real with your pain for the truth to be revealed, so you can be healed.* Burying just places it somewhere unseen, but that does not mean it can't be found when you go digging.

My choosing to reject my own heart by not taking time to mourn and process through loss, but instead to bury and scurry is part of why my cycles continued to happen in all relationships even after discovering the truth from those journals. I was not dealing with the root of why I was doing what I was doing in the first place. I was not changing emotionally or spiritually, so nothing in the physical was changing either. Until I chose to love myself enough by becoming vulnerable and go after what lied underneath; deep down inside me, nothing was going to change. I did not begin learning lessons in life, which increased my knowledge and wisdom and produced change until I allowed my pride to take a back seat, became vulnerable and took a hard look at myself. Until that happened, I continued to walk in my stupid and far away from breakthrough and inner transformational healing.

A New Cycle

Choosing not to forgive basically says... They owe me a debt when Jesus already paid for it all. That was a hard one to swallow, but very necessary for me to receive the healing so I could move forward out of my past and into total freedom. I discovered that forgiveness is for me not the other person. I also chose to release all judgement, because it is not my job to judge but only Gods. Instead of resentment and blame, I chose to forgive and show grace. Instead of judgment, I chose mercy. By choosing forgiveness, I invited God and the power of the cross into the situation and He began pulling up those seeds of hurt, anger, bitterness and pain within my heart and soul. These new seeds of forgiveness and love over time began growing, and I soon began reaping the benefits of those new divine seeds. These new and much improved divine seeds produced life within me and silenced the darkness inside and the enemy's hand on my life. These new seeds began producing new fruits and as these new fruits began growing in size and quantity, freedom too began to grow, mature and produce more healthy crops of freedom. This became my new cycle of renewing and re-strengthening not only my mind, but my heart, spirit and soul as well.

Soil conditions

Mark 4: 14- 20: "The farmer sows the word. Some people are like seed along the path, where the word is sown. As soon as they hear it, Satan comes and takes away the word that was sown in them. Others, like seed sown on rocky places, hear the word and at once receive it with joy. But since they have no root, they last only a short time. When trouble or persecution comes because of the word, they quickly fall away. Still others, like seed sown among thorns, hear the word; but the worries of this life, the deceitfulness of wealth and the desires for other things come in and choke the word, making it unfruitful. Others, like seed sown on good soil, hear the word, accept it, and produce crop some thirty, some sixty, some a hundred times what was sown."

The above scripture is referred to as The Parable of The Sower and was a very important story that Jesus told at the beach in Galilee before a large crowd of people. This parable is also written about in Matthew 13:1-23 and Luke 8:4-15. So that has me believe that (1) Matthew, Mark and Luke were all present at the beach listening to the parable and (2) all three must have recognized the value of it in life to document it. Before I personally understood my true God-given identity, I heard this verse many times but never truly understood the meaning of it. I had no idea that Jesus was referring to the condition of our hearts, spirit and soul. I'll explain it like I now see it from my own life's experiences.

- The hard ground represents someone with a hardened heart full of sin that hears the word of God but does not accept it. Satan can keep this person from growing at all. *(The more you nourish your heart with hate, bitterness, unforgiveness and resentment the further away you are from God because He is love and opposes hate, the two totally clash. In addition, fear of being hurt protected my heart believing it might happen again and kept God out too).*

- The stony ground is someone who shows interest and awareness in the Gospel, yet his heart isn't fully convicted so that when trouble comes his faith is not strong enough to stand. *(I like to refer to this as "straddling the fence" I wanted to be good and do as God said; more out of duty, but there was this part of me that couldn't quite get there completely and kept sabotaging anything good in my life, believing that I didn't deserve it. I lived my life like I was on a teeter-totter on steroids, good than bad, good than bad, good than bad, living from shame and self-condemnation, God was there if I needed Him when I was in distress but when times were good, not so much).*

- The thorny ground is a person who receives the Gospel but who has many other idols and distractions in life - worries, riches, and lusts, which take over his mind and heart and he cannot grow in the truth of God's Word. *(This for me is when I chose to worship another God: relationships with men, sex or lustful thoughts. I felt too ashamed and unworthy to approach God, so I didn't. God only favored the sinless).*

- The good soil is someone who has heard and received the Word of God and allows it to take root and grow within his life. This person represents true salvation that bears good fruit. *(It wasn't until I died completely of me and my junk that I was able to see clearly His truth and not only see and hear it but accept and receive it within. It was my choice to make this transfer of my spirit and soul from death to life and was not due to a need to people please but just to please God).*

One of the main reasons I continued to cycle around was due to the condition of my heart, mind, soul and spirit. The foundation of each was not established in truth but in false beliefs and lies. A farmer is very concerned about the soil in his fields because he realizes the healthier the soil, the healthier the crop. Since the soil of my heart, mind and spirit was not in a healthy state, I was continuing to produce unhealthy outcomes in my life. There was no way I would be able to truly hear and accept the word of God without first taking care of the condition of my soil. Due to my lifestyle choices, my soil was contaminated, and this contamination was doing just that in my life.

In addition; when we plant seeds of judgment against our parents, siblings, friends, neighbors, bosses, pastors, the church and God; we will reap judgment and that too can be seen in the condition of our harvest.

Bible fact: *The word seed is mentioned 349 times and soil is mentioned 114 times in the bible which tells me that God is serious when it comes to our soil, our sowing and what we are reaping.*

The best way to determine the condition of your soil and the seeds you are sowing is to look at the harvest you are producing today in your life. Take time to consider the following:

What fruit am I harvesting at this present time in my life?

Relationally – (successful or unsuccessful marriages or friendships)

Physically – (Healthy or unhealthy)

Financially – (Wealthy or poor; Surplus or living paycheck to paycheck; employed or unemployed)

Emotionally – (Content or troubled; Happy or depressed; Positive or Negative; Always offended or easy going)

Ask yourself the below questions and take time to think about each one. There is zero judgment or shame so relax and trust in the process. Even if you have cycles and mountains you are continuing to circle around, God already knows that and loves you regardless of those cycles!

As you begin reflecting so to answer the below questions, challenge yourself to engage with your inner child so you will view things from the perspective of you as a child not an adult. The adult in us will try to rationalize things instead of deal with it, especially if you are analytical. The adult will try to make excuses or even brush it off as nonsense. And if you are fearful of feeling or believe feelings are bad like I did, you might be very uncomfortable with feelings so try and bypass it all together. Jesus is interested in healing the wounded and broken child within you so you can be set free in your adult body and not be led by the wound(s) anymore.

1. What emotion was nurtured in your home when you were young?

2. What was the atmosphere like in your home?

3. How did your parents handle conflict and stress?

4. How was love demonstrated to you from your dad? Your mom? Siblings?

5. How did you see love as a child?

6. How was love demonstrated between your parents?

7. Did you have a safe place to go when upset?

8. As a child, did you need to hide to be safe?

9. If you had siblings, how did they treat you?

10. Did you think one of your siblings to be favored over the others?

11. Were you punished even when you were innocent?

12. Did you receive protection from your father?

13. Was your dad a good provider?

14. Were you given the opportunity to go after your own dreams?

15. Were you allowed to speak your mind?

16. Did you need to grow up too early due to the irresponsibility of your parents?

17. Were you subjected to any form of abuse by your parents, siblings or another family member? (Physical, emotional, sexual).

18. Was either of your parents emotionally unpredictable where walking on eggshells became part of your daily routine?

19. Were you forced to do things when you did not want to?

I could go on and on because it is so easy to judge others especially when they have hurt us, and we feel we are treated unfairly and did not get justice for what we believe deserved justice. These are all important questions when diving deep into the maturity of our adult spiritual and emotional self. It is possible that these questions will stir up hidden emotions lying within and that can be very troubling and cause discomfort. The discomfort you might be feeling is the hidden wound that needs to be addressed. Go back and place a check mark next to the questions that stirred an emotional response within you so you can later uncover the hidden wound, and deal with it if you desire to. I always see it as an opportunity for healing and God loving me to wholeness instead of something to fear.

What leads us emotionally as an adult most likely is what was nurtured or not nurtured within us as children. It is very important to recognize the fruit in your life today so you can uncover the seeds that were sown from your childhood, young adult and even your adult-self. *Whatever your life's circumstances are today is a good reflection of those seeds sown from childhood.*

Once again, look at the fruit you are harvesting in your life today. If you struggle in relationships per say, seeds of judgment against friendships or other relationships were most likely planted. This is a tough one to understand but so essential when it comes to breakthrough and freedom. To help, I am going to give you a couple of examples from my own life. (Below is from young Marcia Ann's perspective)

- One of my judgments was against my dad for distancing himself from me and not trying to connect when I was little. He never had time for me and as a little girl, I never once remember sitting in his lap. So, guess what I attracted to me and reaped in my marriages? Men who were unable to connect emotionally and kept themselves busy with work, so I always felt distant from them, rejected and not chosen like I felt with my dad.

- I judged my sisters for betraying and excluding me when we were on vacation when I was 14, so later in life I continued to reap that in my girlfriend relationships. It would never fail that there would be 3 of us who hung out together and somehow, I would be the odd one out; drama would arise and guess who would be offended, feel betrayed and shut down? 10 points for you if you said it was ME!

If you struggle with people gossiping about you, guess what seeds you yourself have sown throughout your life? If you answered, gossip; Ding! Ding! Ding! You are correct! 10 more points! What about finances? Do you struggle staying ahead? There is a good chance you might have judged your own dad or mom for being a penny pincher or not being a good provider. Even what we sow today, we will reap tomorrow. Say you desire more grace and generosity from your spouse, well then begin planting seeds of grace and generosity towards him/her and others. It's really that simple. If we look to others to change instead of looking at ourselves, we will continue going around our mountain and will continue to produce the same ole fruit we have been producing.

"God wants to use you to make other people happy. And the happier you make others; the happier you will be because you reap what you sow." Joyce Meyer

This is not an easy topic to understand but when you do get it, it can transform your life's circumstances and end those cycles. The biggest change in my life happened once I stopped judging and blaming others, became vulnerable with myself and God, and allowed Holy Spirit to be real with me. It was then and only then that my circumstances began changing because His truth was able to come in and transform the condition of my heart, mind and spirit. The truth regarding judgments is that they are ours so we will then reproduce those judgments in all our relationships. I was the one producing those outcomes with the men and women in my life not the other way around.

Before I knew this truth, I blamed the men and women I chose to be in relationship with, shame blames and pride will say it is always the other persons fault. After Holy Spirit showed me this redemptive truth, I repented for the judgments I had made knowingly or unknowingly and began planting new seeds of grace and forgiveness; set healthy boundaries and discovered the beauty of having healthy friendships without betrayal and rejection, not because they changed but because I did. It did require me being aware of my triggers and being vulnerable with my new relationships, so they too knew my struggles and triggers. I became transparent, honest, vulnerable and open to the loving correction from Holy Spirit and those I had a relationship with. I established accountability people in my life that loved me enough to hold me accountable for my actions. In other words, I became humble not prideful. I took responsibility for my choices and judgments instead of blaming everyone else for the fruit of my harvest.

As I yearned for Jesus, I learned from Jesus.

Marcia Ann Congdon

Once all my blinders had been removed, I was so ready and open for this type of teaching from Holy Spirit. I was so over my cycles and circling around my mountain yet again and so yearned for more of this type of knowledge and wisdom because I knew it would eventually change my outcomes. I have discovered that yielding and yearning are two beautiful words of surrender. *As I yearned for Jesus, I learned from Jesus.* There was learning produced from my times of yearning and yielding to His promptings and His guidance as He led me into His arms and into total freedom.

If you checked any of the questions earlier; I want to encourage you to forgive those that might have caused you harm; once again from your child's heart, and release all judgment of them back to God where the judgment belongs. It is important to recognize that sometimes it can be our perspective and harm was not intended by the person we judged. And there might be times, that the intention of the person was to harm us and still, it is not our place to judge. Once again, the goal is for you to be free and for you to enter a deeper and more meaningful connection with your heavenly family. We can only fix and change ourselves.

I have included a prayer below if you choose to forgive and release judgment.

Father, today I choose to forgive _____ for _____. *(Be specific here with why you need to forgive). I choose today to release all judgement I have made against _____. Please bless _____ and protect them from harm. Please Jesus, help me through this since I know I cannot do this alone and I need your guidance and strength to get me though. Please forgive me for hanging onto this unforgiveness for so long and for any judgement I wrongly made against them due to my pain. Please release the pain from within my body that I chose to hang onto and restore my body by breathing life back into it. I ask this in the mighty and powerful name of Jesus, Amen.* (Repeat this prayer for each person you need to forgive and release judgement of).

If there is a pain in your past that you cannot revisit, please don't. It's okay and you can ask for assistance. You know yourself better than anyone else. However, I do want to encourage you to seek out a Professional Christian Counselor, Inner Healing Specialist or Pastor and ask them to help guide you through the processing of your pain and then through these prayers so you can receive healing and be able to release the person(s) who harmed you so they no longer have power over you. My email is on the back of this book if you even wanted to reach out to me. The goal is to be free.

5 HANDCUFFED TO SHAME

A fter I became pregnant with my son, I felt so ashamed of everything; the beginning, the middle and the end. I went into a dark pit of shame without really being aware of that fact since shame itself is quite deceptive. It's not like I could visibly see it lurking around the corner ready to pounce on me. Shame is different from guilt because shame takes a direct hit at you, as a person where guilt focuses more on your behavior. Instead of viewing the behavior I demonstrated as bad, I viewed myself as bad. As I unknowingly gave permission for shame to come in and rent space in my brain, my heart and soul; my perspective of myself and life in general was first filtered through my lens of shame and then my actions followed suit. I began seeing and hearing things from inside my pit's perspective and from there, things were very dark and gloomy. I began believing that I no longer deserved happiness because I blew my chances of it due to my sinful behavior and choices I had made, and bad people don't deserve good things.

I believed that I was a bad person and since I also believed God to be an angry God, a punisher, not a lover; He would now punish me for all my bad choices and behaviors and so for 30 years, I lived out life from a damaged soul, and not because God was punishing me, but because I was punishing myself. In a nutshell, I chose to become a prisoner to shame and punishment. I even began believing that there were no second chances and that I would now have to just settle for scraps which is what I also deserved. I truly believed this and the shame, victim and orphan in me supported those beliefs and pride made sure to keep me there.

I locked away all my childhood dreams of a loving and happy marriage securely in a cage and threw away the key. I married my sadness, shame and pain and had babies of regret, bitterness and hopelessness. It was also shame that kept me from even dealing with or talking about my past due to believing that if I removed my fig leaf and became vulnerable; sharing the truth about my past, what happened and how I was truly feeling, people would judge me and too discover just how bad of a person I really am.

Keeping things locked away inside does one thing and one thing only, eat away at your inner core of reality and truth and far away from emotional and spiritual healing and maturity. There is no way I could truly enter freedom by being only partially vulnerable and humble. I had to commit 100% of myself to God and give Him full permission to uncover the ugliness inside me; face it, process through it and hand it over to Him. Then and only then could I begin the rebuilding and restoring process alongside Him. The junk had to come out first before His living waters could flow back in. *"Out with the old, in with the new."*

The bible says *"and the truth will set you free"* and it wasn't until I completely humbled myself, every square inch of me; gave Jesus all my shame and pain inside, recognized Jesus as my one and only God, and spoke His absolute truth back into me; no matter how uncomfortable it made me, is when I began to experience what true transformation and freedom felt like. The key here for me was seeing myself worthy of His truth and this required my perspective to change because if I continued to choose to flow in and from victim, orphan or shame, I would never see myself worthy, capable, loved, significant, or valued because victim, orphan and shame tell you otherwise.

It was when I chose to accept Jesus, ALIVE within me, not just as my savior, but my husband and best friend is when all those blinders became dismantled and I was then able to recognize some hard truths;

1. God does not create victims so if I was choosing a victim mindset, I was going against God as my Creator and basically saying indirectly to Him that He did not do a good job when He created me. *Romans 8:37NIV - No, in all these things we are more than conquerors through him who loved us.*

2. God came for me which means He chose me and did not leave me as an orphan. If I continued to partner with an orphan mindset or was still looking to be chosen by a man, I was once again calling God and His word, (Jesus) a liar. *John 14:18NIV- I will not leave you as orphans; I will come to you.*

3. If I was living in fear, whether fear of failure, fear of man, fear of being hurt, or fear of letting my guard down so I could love or be loved; I was still not understanding the perfect love of God because His perfect love casts out all fear. *1 John 4:18NIV - There is no fear in love. But perfect love drives out fear, because fear has to do with punishment. The one who fears is not made perfect in love.*

4. If I was uncomfortable with love, then I was uncomfortable with God for God IS LOVE. *1John 4:7 NIV - Beloved, let us love one another, for love is from God, and whoever loves has been born of God and knows God.*

What you will read below I kept a secret until the writing of this book. I never spoke of it because I was so ashamed of my decisions leading up to this scenario. I was terrified that if everyone knew the truth, they would no longer like me just like I didn't like me. When Jesus comes in and you allow His truth to fill all the emptiness inside you, truth is something you welcome because it represents who He is. And I will say this again, until I changed, nothing changed, and part of my inner change required me being humble, vulnerable and dealing with my inner turmoil.

Now that the lawyers were handling everything, I no longer felt that I could speak up and to be honest, I don't think I knew how to. If I did have the opportunity to speak what was on my heart, I would have tried to persuade my dad to just drop the case and allow me to take care of my baby alone. I don't need child support or help, and I don't want it! The truth was that I knew my secret and wanted to keep it that way. From my 18-year old's pregnant perspective, I had enough to deal with already! Besides being 18 and pregnant, I was confused, ashamed, nauseous, irritable, fatigued and extremely scared of what was happening so just give me a flipping break! Shame felt like this heavy cloud that weighed down upon my head and shoulders 24/7. Everywhere I went, I believed that everyone that looked at me instantly knew that I was a dirty person, pregnant out of wedlock, a sinner and a huge disgrace to her family. I gave so much power to these thoughts, perspectives and at times they determined my mood for the day and my thoughts of the future.

I did not live then; I survived, one day to the next filled with fear, shame, guilt and regret, believing that if my family knew the truth about me, they would hate me as much as I hated me. If I took time to think about my life in detail and how it was turning out; it would overwhelm me, so I tried my hardest to bury and steer away from those painful and in many ways' traumatic thoughts. The amount of guilt and shame never let up, not even after my son was born; mainly due to believing I was a dirty and a sinful person rather than being a single mom.

I loved my son and lavished him with as much love as I could possibly give and for a time it helped ease my pain, it was nice to be needed by the little fella. At least, someone was choosing me. He became my world and in a sense my God and I loved spending every waking hour with him and if I could have, would have stayed at home instead of worked. Since I carried so much guilt and shame, I felt bad about that too and feared that he possibly would grow up believing his grandma was his mom, not me. Shame and fear played a role in pretty much every area of my life and I just couldn't shake it no matter how much I tried, mainly because I was unaware it even existed. I was even ashamed of my body now since I had a few stretch marks on my lower belly so that too I viewed as bad and dirty and in many ways' punishment for my sinfulness. As I peered into my mirror at home what I saw gazing back at me was a terrible, sinful, dirty person who has messed up her life and the lives of her parents and Prince. I had no idea that I was giving myself a whole lot of power by believing I affected that many lives. I did not see someone who was strong, determined, a fighter, an overcomer and a good mom. The lens I looked through had a huge layer of shame smeared all over it, so this kept me from seeing clearly.

The lawyers scheduled a day for me, my son and Prince to have our blood drawn for the paternity test. As the day drew near, I just couldn't take the guilt and shame anymore so decided to come clean with my secret to my dad. When I sat down with him and told him that there was the possibility Prince was not the father, his response was... "So how many other guys have you slept with?" I knew he was right and believed I deserved that response. I did not need him to tell me he was disappointed or disgusted in me; I knew he was. I went into my natural response of repeated "I'm sorry's" and "Please forgive Me's." I eventually retreated to my room and resumed my mommy duties hoping that would erase some of the additional guilt and shame I was now feeling.

There was a part of me that felt less burdened now that I had revealed my secret to my dad but that did not ease the fear I had, knowing that the results could possibly not go in my favor and I would lose my Prince and my dreams forever. I loved my son regardless of who his dad was but deep inside, desired it to be the boy I loved with all my heart.

The day had come for our blood tests and as I carried my son who was 6 months old down the hospital hallway, there walking towards us was Prince and his parents. My heartbeat raced because there he was; my Prince, the love of my life walking towards me. I had not seen or spoken to him since that night in his bedroom almost 14 months earlier. He had not changed one bit and I so longed that I could run up to him, hug him, feel his arms around me and everything be okay. The pain I felt that day in the hospital hallway is something I will never forget. As they slowly walked past us, Prince quickly glanced at me with a blank expression and I mouthed the words, "I'm sorry." He made no acknowledgment and his parents completely ignored me and my heart ached more. This was all my fault and I could not change or fix it and that too plagued me. I had made one big mess of everything!

It was a month later before the results came back. My dad received the call from our attorney and scheduled an appointment for us to go see him in person to hear the results. I sat in our attorney's office alongside my dad and wished I was not born. I hated every part of my existence and this day was no different. To be perfectly honest, the only reason I had for living was for my son. My young 19-year-old self believed I had caused so many people pain and was not dealing with it well. Our attorney looked at me and my dad; fiddled with the papers and regretfully announced that my Prince was not my son's father. The moment those words left his mouth, it felt like my heart, hopes and dreams; what was left of them shattered into a zillion pieces. I had never shared with the attorney the possibility of my son not being Princes and I'm not sure if my dad did either, so I felt such embarrassment knowing I not only was a disappointment to my dad, but a disappointment to my lawyer as well. I believed he too viewed me as this horrible, bad person who was now, also a big fat liar. I seriously wanted to crawl into a giant hole and never come out again. I also knew that my Prince and his parents were hearing the same news at their attorney's office and were most likely celebrating. I was so embarrassed, so ashamed, so sad.

I also knew for certain that I would never see or talk to my Prince again or his parents who I had grown to also love and that broke my heart. Just like that, any possibility of life with him was gone and so were my dreams. The amount of grief I was feeling at that very moment was overwhelming to say the least and I had no idea how to cope with everything rising within me, so I did what I knew and buried it all. The drive home was miserable, and I sat in silence and in shame. I did make one decision and that was to never ever believe in love, fairytales or happy endings again; they were all shams, hoaxes and facades.

I see shame like a plague. It cannot be seen with the physical eye and its mission is to destroy whatever gets in its path. Shame takes part in the destruction of hopes and dreams of a better future. Shame says you are altogether bad and everything you do is bad. Shame, if left unchecked and dealt with can continue to keep you in your past and so that is where you will continue to live from and far away from Gods plans for you, and God's perspective of you. Gods' plans talk of a future that is good, prosperous and filled with hope and shame won't allow that to happen. Until we partner and see ourselves as God does, we will not be able to enter the plans He has for us.

Shame instead wants you to give up and throw in the towel on what you once held dear to your heart because you are too bad to deserve anything good. Shame needs to breed more shame to prove its point that you are bad and unworthy of good things in life, and pride will convince you that you are right and deserve what you have coming.

While I was still walking in and from shame one of my favorite scripture verses was *Jeremiah 29:11 and I could even quote it for you. For I know the plans I have for you," declares the LORD, "plans to prosper you and not to harm you, plans to give you hope and a future.* I had this one verse all around my house as a reminder of just how good God is.   However, I was completely unaware at that time that there was no way I truly understood how good God was if I was still walking in victim and shame.   Both involve punishment and fear and God is perfect love, a noun not a verb. Shame and victim involve condemnation where Gods love deals with grace and forgiveness and leads you into ultimate freedom. I could quote that scripture all I wanted, but for me to come into agreement with it and have it rooted within me, I was going to first need to deal with all my shame and hidden pain. The truth is that there is no way I could even declare that scripture as truth if I was still living from an orphan, victim, slave or shame mindset and perspective. The only way I was going to see God's plans for me fulfilled in my lifetime was if I chose to walk in fullness as His chosen daughter; not a victim, an orphan or slave which meant seeing me as He saw me through a pure lens not one filtered first through my broken-mess.

Chain breaking truth

If I would have not followed the promptings of The Holy Spirit; gotten very uncomfortable and dug deep into inner healing of

my younger self, I would have not discovered this chain-breaking truth I am about to share. As the above memory played out in my mind, I knew that there was a very good chance that I had not loved myself well and therefore abandoned my 19-year-old just like I had my 7-1/2 and 18-year old by not showing myself grace or giving myself permission to process through the losses and pain I felt back then, but instead stuffed it all away and pretended I was okay.

Sure enough; when The Holy Spirit led me back into this memory so I could love myself back to wholeness, I discovered my 19-year old self still hunkered down in the corner of the lawyers office; overwhelmed with fear, shame, embarrassment and an over-all sense of being a letdown as a daughter to her dad. What I discovered was just how similar my feelings and my postures were with each painful memory I chose to revisit, so I could retrieve my younger self out of her broken-mess and experience inner freedom today as a 56-year old.

Each time, whether in the bathroom stall, the dark and rainy woods, the church parking lot, or the Lawyers office; as I allowed my younger self to feel, (not shut her down because my adult-self was uncomfortable), and have a voice, what I recognized with each; my 7-1/2 year old, 18 and 19-year old was that they all expressed being afraid, rejected, ashamed, abandoned, not heard and an overwhelming sense of being a *letdown as a daughter*.

Nothing had changed with my outcomes today, because nothing had changed within me. The lies I believed as truth were dictating who I believed I was and what treatment in life I deserved. I had not loved on myself enough to process through my loss, fear, grief or any other feelings since I believed my feelings to be bad, just like I was, and too painful to deal with and in a sense feared feeling. I shutdown and shutoff instead of loving myself through the process. I did the exact thing to me that I blamed others for. By not processing and loving myself through the pain, I was rejecting, abandoning, betraying and disconnecting from myself.

As I entered the Lawyer's office, my heart ached as I saw her sobbing in the corner. Jesus and I slowly and gently approached her and asked if we could sit down and she shook her head, yes. I immediately sensed that she knew who we were from the other encounters and so the introduction phase was not necessary. Before I even asked her if I could hug her, she fell into my arms and began weeping. I cried along with her as I stroked her hair and held her close like a momma would her sick child. I apologized to her for abandoning her once again and would she forgive me? Her tears began to subside and so I asked if she would like to share how she was feeling because we were here for her because we loved her.

She began explaining just how terrible she felt for disappointing and embarrassing her dad the way she did in front of the lawyer. She then said...." I am such a letdown as a daughter!" She also shared the amount of guilt she was experiencing knowing that she caused pain and drama for Prince and His family by lying in the first place. She knew she had let them down as well and that too she took to heart and it plagued her. I sat and listened, validated and empathized with her and when she was ready, guided her through forgiveness prayers of herself so that she could leave that Lawyer's office free of any shame, self-condemnation, guilt, and even self-hate once and for all.

Both Jesus and I encouraged her to say good-bye to the pain, the embarrassment, shame and feelings of disappointment or being a failure, and to not choose to own them has her identity anymore.

She obliged and decided to forgive herself and break any and all agreements she had made that day with the lies of being stupid, an embarrassment and a letdown to her dad, the lawyer and Prince and his parents.

She motioned to get up and as we exited the lawyers office together and turned the corner into the hallway, we were no longer standing within a building, we were standing on a beautiful beach, the sun hitting our faces, seagulls soaring above us, we were laughing, dancing and splashing in the waves and I knew the healing transformation was complete.

It was not until this 4th memory and interaction I had with my younger self that I realized the root which was that I believed I was a letdown as a person in general and as a daughter to my dad, and I identified myself as a *letdown,* so that is exactly what I became and produced throughout my life. I produced it with my teacher, Prince, both sets of parents, (mine and Princes), my marriages, my friendships, work relationships, my children and even myself.

I also believed I was a letdown to God and that kept me from intimate connection with Him, especially seeing Him as a Father and me a daughter. Yes, I struggled with other identity issues and negative outlooks of myself, but the big mama-jama was that one word – *"LETDOWN!"* What a huge release I felt from deep down within me when I came out of agreement with that one word. The *chain-breaking truth* was that I was not a letdown to Jesus, God or Holy Spirit, and I never have been and that was all that mattered. I chose to love myself well, so decided to no longer give so much power over to that one word and the lie it produced within me, and everything began to change because I changed what I was agreeing with and what was leading my thoughts and actions.

Changing perspectives

A couple of years ago, my husband and I had a very large and beautiful willow tree suddenly fall in our front yard. At first, I was devastated because I loved that tree and I so enjoyed gazing upon its beauty every morning when I woke up. When my husband began cutting the tree up, he noticed that the core of the tree was filled with disease. I immediately heard Holy Spirit say to me, "See, even though it was so beautiful on the outside, inside it was broken." Wow! That was me when I was flowing in shame and pain! On the outside, I looked great but, on the inside, I was a broken and shame-filled mess. All that stuffing, burying and scurrying had taken quite a toll on my heart and soul. That is what shame and hidden painful wounds can do to our insides when left unchecked and not properly dealt with. From that place of brokenness or shall I say **broken-mess** I was making terrible choices for myself which didn't just impact my life but so many others around me as well.

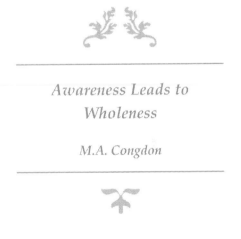

Awareness Leads to Wholeness

M.A. Congdon

In my quest for complete inner healing I have discovered that Holy Spirit, Jesus and God love me so much that they too did not want me to remain in my brokenness so lovingly and patiently brought me face to face with my inner broken-mess, so they could not only establish truth within my spirit, soul and body, but place me on a new pathway leading to ultimate freedom in Christ. I had to first become aware; not only of their infinite and non-judgmental, grace-filled love, but the necessity and importance of loving myself enough to open up and believe I not only am worthy of this form of love, but deserve it as well.

As Jesus healed and mended the broken places within me, my perspectives of myself changed and therefore my perspectives of God, Jesus and Holy Spirit changed. As this inner transformation took place, I was able to begin seeing myself from Gods perspective, not my own and not mans. I was able to begin welcoming His truth and allowed this amazing form of love to retrieve the pain, and then trust as He released His healing truth within the areas now ready to welcome and receive it. *I had to first become aware before God could set things in motion that would bring about the transformation process of my mind, spirit and soul.*

Through this transformational inner healing journey, Holy Spirit continues to remind me that *Awareness leads to wholeness* so to this day, I pray for my heavenly counselors to bless me with spiritual wisdom so I can remain *aware* of any hidden sadness, regret, judgement, pain, anger, fear, neglect or unforgiveness left in my heart still lurking inside, knowing that when it is brought to the light, healing is there waiting to be grabbed ahold of and taken in.

I personally would not change a thing about this time in my cocoon; churning and turning things upside down and inside out within me in order to get to those ugly seeds and roots where shame and pain were birthed. I am grateful for that time because it resulted in discovering the true Agape love of Jesus which led me out of darkness and into wholeness. I discovered that He has always loved me even in my ugliness because He never saw the ugliness, because He cannot recognize something within us that is not within

Him. I hope you got that. Jesus mirrors back to His Father perfection because His Father is perfect and if God created us in His image than He sees us perfect too. If we mirror back brokenness, then our eyes are not set on God but instead on the brokenness of whomever we have made God.

It was that type of spiritual wisdom from The Father's heart that produced transformation within me because it shifted my internal lenses and I suddenly became aware of my inner beauty as seen from the eyes of my loving heavenly Father and no longer from my brokenness. Things came into focus and for the first time, I was able to see myself as His handiwork, His princess instead of someone who had let Him down, is sinful and dirty. From there, I understood the importance of showing grace to myself by loving myself regardless of my past mistakes and thereby opened myself up even more to learning how to partner with His truth, grace and mercy; see it as love even though at times it hurt going deep, trust for a change knowing that His love is perfect and fear had to be a thing of the past, not the present.

Another truth came into focus and that was; if I mistreated myself and at the same time believed that Jesus lived within me, then I was mistreating Him as well. Mistreatment includes shaming, judging, rejecting, shutting down, angry at, resenting, bad-mouthing myself, dishonoring, disrespecting, etc., etc. Like I just mentioned above; God made us in His own image, so once again we are disapproving of God Himself and His handiwork when we mistreat ourselves.

Genesis 1:27NIV – So God created mankind in his own image, in the image of God he created them; male and female he created them.

I love the following quote and now can see how it played out in my own life while on this journey of mending and *reparenting* my heart, spirit and soul. *"Butterflies can't see their wings. They can't see how truly beautiful they are."* I have discovered that as I allowed the truth serum of heaven to seep into every area of my spirit, soul and body, and as it washed away all my pain and shame, I was able to see others from a place of love and grace instead of through my filter of pain, fear and shame.

Pain smeared an ugly film over my perspective of myself, God and other people's intentions towards me which hindered my ability to see things from a place of love, not shame or fear. As I allowed Jesus in to heal my pain and reintroduce me to His perfect love; fear began slowly becoming less relevant and as that happened, my perspective shifted with this newfound freedom. I had no idea how imprisoned I was to fear until I began discovering the truth about Gods perfect love; outside of my religious beliefs and upbringing. To say it was an eye-opening experience is an understatement.

God is a God of sifting, shifting and shaking and as I gave Him permission to sift, shift and shake away, many chains of brokenness and shackles of pain of the past shattered into a million pieces as they dropped to the ground. There is no way the enemy can stay when you know the truth of God's perfect love for you. He's going to try his darndest, but when your shield is your faith in God's goodness and your sword is the word of God, he doesn't stand a chance. Once I made the choice to step out of my own bondage and what was initially holding me back and instead chose to step into victory, which is what Gods word speaks of, change began happening in and around me.

Ephesians 6: 14-17NIV - Stand firm then, with the belt of truth buckled around your waist, with the breastplate of righteousness in place, and with your feet fitted with the readiness that comes from the gospel of peace. In addition to all this, take up the shield of faith, with which you can extinguish all the flaming arrows of the evil one. Take the helmet of salvation and the sword of the Spirit, which is the word of God.

I had to see myself healed, see myself as a finished work of His art, and see myself pure, restored and redeemed by His blood for my life circumstances to change too. I cannot say that enough and with the conviction I feel as I am writing this. The change came when I changed my perspective of God, myself, and Christ within me. If Christ lives in me; how can I then think I am ugly, impure, bad, shameful and unworthy? I am calling Christ those same things as well and that my friends will please the accuser but grieve the Holy Spirit. How can I say I am a new creation, created in likeness of Jesus and then believe those lies about myself? There is no way I can say with certainty that I am saved, healed and delivered and live my life from a place of orphan, victim or slave perspectives.

How can I then be a witness to others of Gods goodness, His faithfulness, if I am still living from those perspectives or mindsets? I am then still living in my old wine skins and my bones are still dead so how am I appearing to non-believers? Who would want to follow a God that does not take care of His children? If the bible says the old is dead and I am a new creation, then that means everything about me is new and everything I did in the past is dead. God is not the one digging my old self back up from the grave, I was. If I continued to dwell on my past and mull over it, whatever verses I was quoting from the bible were not grabbing ahold of me internally. I might have sounded all Christian-like, but my insides and my actions showed differently.

2 Corinthians 5:17 NLT - This means that anyone who belongs to Christ has become a new person. The old life is gone; a new life has begun!

Mark 2:22 NLT - "And no one puts new wine into old wineskins. For the wine would burst the wineskins, and the wine and the skins would both be lost. New wine calls for new wineskins."

The Beauty of Vulnerability

The first time God showed me that choosing to exist from a place of shame ultimately even damaged the word, *"Intimacy,"* I found myself alongside 3 other ministers, lined up in front of a church one evening in South Georgia. The four of us had driven down that day completely unaware that we would be leading church later that evening, but God did. My ministry partner and dear friend was sitting next to me and led things off. She had written the word *"Intimacy"* on a pink sticky note and showed it to me. As I got a glimpse of the word, I physically felt repulsed, my insides cringed, and anxiety began rising within me. It was at that moment Holy Spirit began showing me why the word triggered me and gently encouraged me to share this with the congregation when it was my turn. It was one of the first times I allowed myself to be fully vulnerable and transparent in front of a group of strangers and this choice gave permission for God to go deeper and get through some additional layers I was unaware of at that time. I love how He loves me so perfectly well; He is such a great Dad!

As my dear friend began the discussion by sharing the beauty of intimacy with Jesus, my blood felt like it was boiling. My insides were twisting and turning, and I knew something big was about to happen because I could feel the power of God flowing through me.

When it became my turn to share, I knew that I had to be as open, real and honest because that is what Holy Spirit asked of me and I trusted Him. This was not about me; this was about God and bringing Him glory. I was nervous, but I did it anyway. I remember at one point saying…. "The only intimacy I knew was in between the bedsheets." I went on to share with them the real reason I had trouble engaging and initially becoming intimate with Jesus was because that word became a very bad word and involved a great deal of sex, pain and shame in my life. I openly shared with them a memory I had of the first time someone had told me that Jesus wanted to have a personal, intimate relationship with me and how hearing that had repulsed me and triggered anxiety to rise up because to me; that word meant something very ugly, dirty and shameful and scared the bejeebers out of me. What I heard was Jesus wants to inflict pain upon you, hurt you and then leave because intimacy, sex, pain and abandonment were one in the same to me. That entire hidden trauma within me wanted to be heard that night and for the first time, I allowed a hidden pain of my past to have a voice and I stepped into the doorway of healing that opened before me.

It was that very night in a small church in Southern, Georgia that God, Holy Spirit and Jesus teamed up to help guide me through the removal of many masks that I had grown quite comfortable wearing to cover up the pain still lurking inside. As I openly shared my past from a place of love and grace, not shame or hate; internal wreckage was being removed and His joy was released from the His throne of grace straight into the core of my existence. I could personally feel my heart dancing with gladness even though I was revealing a side of myself I had never revealed before.

How freeing vulnerability and transparency is when you are seeking inner transformation and breakthrough. I believe it is the gateway to both.

That night was just the beginning of understanding just how a life of sexual immorality tainted, confused and destroyed many simple words and displays of affection for me. As I opened my heart that night in obedience, many other doors opened as well and I was flooded with wisdom, understanding, knowledge and truth straight from The Father's heart to mine.

He never lets up and I never want Him to because of the freedom each nugget of truth produces within my heart, spirit and soul. I see myself as a sponge soaking up every bit of heavenly wisdom I can get and what a difference it has made internally within me and around me. From that day forward I considered myself an A+ student of Holy Spirits and He began showing me what other words triggered me and why. I discovered that even words like "I love you"; "Trust me" and "I'm Sorry" caused me discomfort and anxiety. Those three simple sentences to me meant the opposite of their true meaning, could not be trusted and were methods of entrapment and manipulation. You see, due to the many years the word love was abused whether by my choices or at the hands of others, sadly to this day, I at times struggle believing the person on the other end speaking them out.

It's an ongoing battle of my mind to almost naturally first revisit the thoughts and feelings of uncertainty, trauma, fear, manipulation and control that surround this word *love* to me. I will hear the words of love and affirmation which most people long to hear, but my brain has been programmed to see a danger sign and before I know it, my heart will put up a road block to keep those emotions at bay and my body responds with anxiety. What my heart and brain hear is; "Danger Will Robinson!" or "Run Forrest Run!" Even though I desired and deep down needed to hear someone tell me they loved me, the moment the words left their mouth, what my heart and head heard was:

- I am going to control you and you will be my prisoner.
- I will discover the truth about you and not love you anymore.
- I will not approve of you and will need you to change.
- I will blame everything on you even if I am wrong.
- I will betray you, lie to you and hurt your heart.
- I will eventually leave you and when you least expect it.
- I cannot be trusted. - I will throw you under the bus every opportunity I get.
- I will not protect you even if you are being physically hurt.
- I will not have your back.
- I will be the one you need protection from, and no one will believe you.
- I will tell you "I love you" just to get what I want from you.
- I will love you if you do as I say and say as I do.

Since this is what my head and heart heard and grabbed ahold of as truth, I unknowingly reacted outwardly by closing off, assumed a posture of defense and made sure to keep my boxing gloves up and ready to combat anything coming in my corner of the ring. I made sure to keep the one who believed they loved me at a distance emotionally and since I believed that they would eventually hurt me, produced the exact behavior from them I believed I deserved. Remember, we produce in our circumstances what we believe to be true. If I believed and expected to not be chosen, what do you think I produced in my marriages? My friendships? My business relationships? And how about betrayal? If I expected to be betrayed? What do you think I produced with the men in my life? If I expected them to not protect me? What do you think I produced in the relationship? Part of my need to feel protected was for them to choose me, to have my back, and in a sense agree with me. If I expected them to reject me and leave? What scenarios do you think I produced in all my relationships so to prove myself right?

As I remained focus on myself and far away from the truth, I continued to cry wolf believing all men were bad and my heart was hurt, yet again! (Victim) When I finally became awakened to this life-giving truth, I discovered that I produced many of the outcomes in my relationships due to my judgments, beliefs and expectations, not the other way around. For inner healing to erupt from within and then transform my inner spirit and soul, I had to come face to face with my junk, not the other persons. All my finger pointing only kept me in my prison cell of choice. The cell transfer occurred when I chose to look inwards for a change and not outwards. I purchased my gold ticket to freedom the moment I came clean and stopped my merry-go-round of shame and blame, owned my junk and released to Jesus any junk I had taken that was not mine to take. *It is the truth that sets you free not the lies you believe as truth.* There is a big difference.

I have discovered on this beautiful transformation journey I have been on alongside Jesus, Father God and Holy Spirit that when I completely surrendered my brain, spirit, heart, soul and will to God and chose to be vulnerable and obey His promptings, however uncomfortable it made me, He immediately blessed me for doing so. He is a great Dad, so He blesses His children when they obey, simple as that. That night in that small church in South Georgia; when I chose to partner with vulnerability and humility instead of fear of man or pride, whatever remaining traces of shame within me seemed to vanish, because there was no way shame could still hang out when God's redemptive glory and truth was flowing so freely. That one experience made such an impact on the realness of God's healing love for me that I knew in that instant what my ministry, calling and purpose needed to be and not for me, but Him. That is the beauty of God's love for us; it is 100% transformational, intentional, unconditional and totally unpredictable. Gosh, He's Good!

Bible Fact: The number of times the word "love" appears in the Bible varies from 514 to 810 according to translations.

My drug of choice

As I openly share this part of my past with you, it is not to shame myself, play the victim or blame game; dig up old wounds to mull over or judge myself again or anyone else who has traveled down a similar path. I did enough of that over those 30 years to know that doesn't work and only kept me in my pain and away from complete inner healing.

What you feed; Leads. What you nourish, will flourish.

M.A. Congdon

I will however, be blunt and speak the truth in hopes of teaching whoever is reading this what is possible when one chooses to nourish the desires of their flesh instead of the desires of our Father's heart, and when one chooses to believe the lies of this world instead of the truth of His word.

As I personally continued to lick my wounds and nourish my fleshy desires. pursuing those over spiritual ones, my fleshy desires grew and grew and eventually led the show. *"What you feed; leads."* *"What you nourish; will flourish."* I was living a life of lustful pleasure, feeding this demon whenever it was hungry and believed it was a normal way of life. It was not until the writing of this book that Holy Spirit shed light on the fact that I coped with my pain by seeking the excitement new relationships produced, believing it would make my emptiness and pain go away. Since it became an outlet to help me cope, an addiction was birthed.

When He showed me that truth; lightbulbs started going off and for the first time I was no longer confused. For me personally, it was more about the excitement of the hunt not so much the act of sex itself. I could take that or leave it. I loved, needed and thoroughly enjoyed the hunt or to be hunted, either way it was exciting to me. Those initial intense feelings of physical attraction and the endorphins that were being released during the newness of the relationship is what I craved and needed to resuscitate me.

Overtime, the more I fed my flesh and the spirit of shame and lust, the stronger they became and the more they needed to be fed. My flesh and this monster of shame and lust within was soon calling all the shots and that included believing that this behavior of mine was okay and even justified. Since I was unaware of my own power to say *no*; mainly due to being a people pleaser and believing I had the power to hurt them by saying no, (such a lie), I continued to follow through with sex even though many times I had no desire to. It was done more out of duty or obligation, like I owed them, not desire or something I truly wanted.

Like any drug, I experienced side effects, physically and emotionally. I would wake up next to someone I hardly knew feeling discombobulated, hung over and uncomfortable given the situation I found myself in. As the encounter ended and reality set in, the feelings of loneliness were still present along with disgust, shame, guilt and fear. These familiar voices in my head screamed at me; "You disgust me!" "You are such a bad and dirty person!" "How could you do something like this and go to church Sunday?!" "Let's just hope you don't get pregnant!" If I believed I had cut it too close to when I ovulated, I would quickly phone my Gynecologist explaining the situation I found myself in and they would phone in a prescription to my pharmacy for the 'day after pill' which prevented me from getting pregnant. I would then shame myself for possibly ending a pregnancy, tell myself I would never do it again and make all sorts of empty promises.

Like all addictions, denial was a bully and overpowered all rational thinking and truth. I can remember even taking pride in the amount of men I bedded, as if it raised the bar of my level of significance and value as a woman. How crass, yet it was the lie I believed as truth and this deception I believed as truth then contaminated my heart. *My heart produced around me what was contained within it.* That is why the bible says to guard your heart because what we give permission to contaminate our brain will then do the same to our heart and once that happens, the contamination spreads outwards through our actions and can be witnessed in our lifestyle choices and circumstantial outcomes. *Proverbs 4:23NIV - Above all else, guard your heart, for everything you do flows from it.*

If you desire change around you, change what lies within. Trust me when I say that nothing changed until I did, and a big part of that change required me seeing myself, not as bad, a letdown or a failure but as someone capable of greatness because God created me to do great things. *I decided to partner with a Kingdom Mindset so my outcomes would represent His Kingdom, living within me.*

Kingdom Mindsets produce Kingdom Outcomes.

Marcia Ann Congdon

When you are led by lust, shame, rejection and confusion, like I was, you aren't very picky. My desire to be noticed, significant, approved of, accepted and chosen far outweighed my need to be respected and honored. Does this sound harsh? Probably so, but the moment I died of myself and my foolish pride and gave God, Jesus and Holy Spirit permission to be blunt and honest with me, was the moment inner healing and transformation began. Marcia Ann and all her pride had to step out of the way for my heavenly parents to take over and do what they do best; *heal and transform.*

As I gave permission to my Heavenly family to sift through my junk and cleanse me from my past, there was one thing I discovered about myself and it was ugly but necessary to have light shed upon it so I could change. There was no way possible that I loved, respected or honored myself or anyone else for that matter. The level of sexual interaction I had with men, not caring about their age or relationship status, sometimes as a sport or extracurricular activity, (friends with benefits, or one night stands), there's no way possible I could sit here and say I cared about myself, valued myself, honored or loved myself or anyone else, God included. The only person I was fooling was me because I sure was not fooling God.

Pride to me resembles those blinders (blinkers), a horse wears to prevent them from seeing behind them or to the side. Pride will keep us firmly placed within our junk, blinded to all truth which in many cases is staring us smack in the face. The deceiving side of pride is that it tells you that what you are choosing to do is normal and justified. I did what I did without even considering for one second the consequences my actions might produce. It's like my conscious died along with my hope and dreams.

That's why I can say with confidence, that all addictions are selfish. There is no way I was thinking about how my lifestyle choice was affecting anyone else, including myself. This lifestyle choice of mine was destroying my ability to connect and be intimate in a healthy way, which was something I had always desired. I was sabotaging the one thing I desired more than anything and that was to feel love for another and to be loved by someone. I thought I was in pursuit of love and happiness, yet I was destroying my ability to do either.

I can say that now, healed and the other side but while I was flowing in my addiction, I did not see that at all. Everyone else was out to get me and make life difficult for little ole me. I'll repeat what I said earlier; *The truth will set you free not the lie you believe as truth.* How many times I watered down the truth so I could swallow it better. Or added flavor to the lie so it tasted less offensive. Either way, when it went down, what I tasted was bile and bile is what I vomited out all over myself and those around me.

Today I choose to walk in His truth, so I love myself, every part of me, regardless of my past because I know that when I love myself, I love Christ since He lives within me. Today, I recognize that if *I do not believe in love than I cannot possibly believe in God since HE IS LOVE and if I do not believe in God than I cannot believe in the person I am because He created me in His image.* When I finally chose to say farewell to pride and shame, and all its filters and blinders, I then and only then was able to truly see my inner value, beauty and worth.

1 John 4:7NIV - Beloved, let us love one another, for love is from God, and whoever loves has been born of God and knows God. [8] Anyone who does not love does not know God, because God is love.

As I openly become vulnerable with my next story; I can share it with you from a place of total healing, not shame. Thank you, Jesus!! This was a process and one that challenged me throughout the writing of this book. It is not so easy to write out your sinful ways and shortcomings and literally come face to face with them as you read and reread them, but I am to say; it is so worth it when you taste the victory in His redemptive glory.

This story is a part of my life journey and without it; I would not be where I am today and so for that, I am forever grateful. I can see just how God so beautifully and perfectly loved, healed and restored me which brings delight and joy, not shame and condemnation. I highly encourage you to write your story because it opens the door for awareness, healing and restoration. As I wrote and rewrote, Holy Spirit educated, counseled, consoled and loved me in ways I had never been loved before which produced additional healing within me. God is The Healer and Mender of our broken hearts and spirits because He desires us to become all He created us to be. He is a God of the possible not impossible.

It was the year 2001 and my 2nd marriage was ending after 7 years. I did what naturally felt right to me; blamed him for all our problems which helped me feel better about my decision to part ways and then went about trying to fill the new gaping voids within me by imagining life with a new man who would truly love me. Before the i's were dotted or the t's crossed on our divorce papers, I was already on the hunt, scoping out future relationship prospects. For me, this was exhilarating and awakened within me this feeling of importance, acceptance and value that I craved so badly and believed I had not been receiving while married to him.

As men payed interest in me and said so, it felt so good inside and helped me forget about the parts of me that still ached. I continued going to places that I received the most attention and it temporarily fed a void within me that so needed to be fed again. Typically, the clubs and local sports bars were the best locations to fill my need when I was running on empty which was quite often. I wanted to make up for the time I loss while I spent 7 years in what I perceived as a loveless, emotionless marriage and hopefully my true soulmate will come into the picture soon and dull out some of this pain of failure, shame and loneliness I am unable to shake at times.

The weekend was quickly approaching and it was a weekend my youngest was going to be with her dad, so I would have the weekend to myself and there is no way I am spending it all alone because that would be devastating! I've got to find someone that wants to go out to a club or a sports bar if I don't have a date. I went about asking clients, co-workers and friends to see if someone was available to go clubbing and have some fun! Friday night came and went, and my desperation grew. There is no way I am going to miss out on not having any kids here and sit at home all alone with nothing to do.

When Saturday night arrived, I could not stand the feelings of emptiness, loneliness and disappointment any longer so decided to phone a friend who just so happened to work as a bartender at a very fancy country club. She was working that night but invited me to come and visit her and just hang out. I agreed and quickly showered and dressed myself in a super cute outfit with the sexiest shoes I owned and hoped that would get the attention of some handsome fella.

Jackpot! A wedding party was celebrating in the bar area, so I scoped out the prospects standing before me to see which one fit my criteria for that one night. After a few drinks I became very friendly with one of the young groomsmen who earlier caught my eye. After several more drinks we decided to go to the men's bathroom and have sex in one of the stalls. Later, I went to his hotel room for another round and not of drinks. Due to his level of intoxication, he quickly passed out after our sexual encounter was over and I laid there next to him, in the dark hotel room and was consumed with remorse and shame.

I quietly got out of the bed, located my clothes, got dressed and along with the overwhelming sense of shame, regret, guilt and self-disgust, made my way down this fancy hotel hallway. It was my walk of shame. I didn't feel classy, fulfilled, loved, valued or accepted at all! I still felt completely alone and empty inside. I remember telling myself as I walked down the hallway that I was a whore and a worthless piece of crap and I might as well start getting paid for what I was doing. I didn't even make it to my car before the tears came streaming down my face. I managed to drive home, praying to not get pulled over and shaking my head in disbelief of what I just did and why?

Consequences

There are always consequences for our choices and my choosing to live life based in lies I believed as truth and from a place of shame, fear and sexual promiscuity on and off for a period of almost 30 years has many. You cannot defile your body, mind, spirit and soul and expect there to be no future side effects. You cannot bury all your pain or turn your emotions off completely and expect them not to contaminate you internally or externally. You cannot enter a life on the run, not dealing with your inner pain and expect that inner pain to not contaminate your present life. Like any drug, there are always side effects. **Unhealed wounds want to be heard and dealt with and if left unheard will still have a say.** Just because you cannot see them with the physical eye does not mean they are not there, and my actions throughout my 30 years of circling my mountain of shame proves just that. 'Ignorance is bliss' to me means; *stay in your stupid.*

Some of the consequences I am still at times faced with today, as a result of my choosing to remain 30 years living from shame and brokenness are: (*It was my choice to stay there.*)

- I have been divorced 3 times.
- I have 3 children from 3 different fathers.
- I must deal with exes and 2nd wives even with grown children.

- I was unable to fully connect emotionally with any and all my relationships, yet believed it was the other way around. (Shame blames)
- I struggle with feelings of inadequacy, low self-esteem and self-doubt.
- I question many of my decisions.
- I struggle being able to dream or hope at times without feeling some fear.
- I have a hard time stating how I truly feel or expressing what I need.
- I go into survival mode very quickly and self-protect which means walls come up and a safe distance is put in place. (body memory)
- I find it hard to trust and believe people are being sincere and true to their word so continually test them.
- I easily partner with shame and guilt because they are comfortable places for me.
- I still at times struggle having an intimate relationship with my 4th and final husband and push him away when I feel he is getting too close. (Body memory-physical feelings arise of entrapment, suffocation)
- I struggle with PTSD due to my childhood atmosphere along with other traumatic experiences that took place when I flowed in shame. (Body memory)

The sexual and shame-filled journey I chose to be on was carved out from my brokenness, false and faulty belief systems and lies I believed as truth, about myself, God and others. The people I attracted and took advice from were typically ones who also resided in the same world and belief system I lived from which helped me feel better about myself and my choices. These choices I made when living from my brokenness resulted in serious consequences in addition to the ones listed above.

I continued to look for something or someone to fill the void I had deep within, but of course they never did. How could they possibly? That is a lot to ask of someone and a great deal of power I was giving over to them. How could any one person help me feel lovable when I didn't believe I was lovable? That is one unrealistic and unachievable task, expectation and weight to place on someone's shoulders. Since no human is perfect, how can they complete me if they are not complete themselves? Only Jesus can do that.

God, throughout history pursued and used imperfect people to fulfill His promises and His perfect will here on earth.

Back when I was unaware of my true identity and value, I was defined by the number of heads I turned and what others thought and said about me, and today I'm only defined by what my heavenly Dad says, and by that I mean my inner beauty. God does not look upon our outer appearances, only our inner. He also is a God that sees past our mistakes, believes in us and desires for us to see ourselves as He sees us. He is a God of grace, mercy and unconditional love. I not only experienced this firsthand, but as I began studying scripture, recognized this truth played out throughout biblical history. *God continues to pursue and use imperfect*

people to fulfill His promises and His perfect will here on earth. He has always done this because He is not focused on our shortcomings, failures or flaws but on who He created us to be, based solely in selfless love.

The key to unlocking the door to true inner peace and freedom is to see yourself as He does so you begin to mirror back His perspective of you not your own or anyone else's. As I discovered and accepted His Father's heart for me, my empty voids began filling up with the promises and truths of His word and therefore what I mirrored back to myself and others was first filtered through these truths instead of the lies I once believed.

Here are just a few mentioned throughout biblical history that God pursued and used.

- *Abraham -Was old*
- *Elijah – Was suicidal*
- *Samson – Was a womanizer.*
- *Rahab – Was a prostitute.*
- *Samaritan Woman – Divorced.*
- *Noah – Was a Drunk.*
- *Jacob – Was a cheater.*
- *David – Was a murderer and adulterer.*
- *Peter – Denied Christ three times.*
- *Matthew – Tax Collector*
- *Paul – A Pharisee who persecuted Christians before becoming one. (Wrote 13 books in the bible.)*

Romans 8:28NIV - And we know that in all things God works for the good of those who love him, who have been called according to his purpose.

6 MY ENCOUNTER AT THE WELL

John 4: 4-26 NIV - Now he had to go through Samaria. So, he came to a town in Samaria called Sychar, near the plot of ground Jacob had given to his son Joseph. Jacob's well was there, and Jesus, tired as he was from the journey, sat down by the well. It was about noon. When a Samaritan woman came to draw water, Jesus said to her, "Will you give me a drink?" (His disciples had gone into the town to buy food.) The Samaritan woman said to him, "You are a Jew and I am a Samaritan woman. How can you ask me for a drink?" (For Jews do not associate with Samaritans.) Jesus answered her, "If you knew the gift of God and who it is that asks you for a drink, you would have asked him, and he would have given you living water." "Sir," the woman said, "you have nothing to draw with and the well is deep. Where can you get this living water? Are you greater than our father Jacob, who gave us the well and drank from it himself, as did also his sons and his livestock?" Jesus answered, "Everyone who drinks this water will be thirsty again, but whoever drinks the water I give them will never thirst. Indeed, the water I give them will become in them a spring of water welling up to eternal life." The woman said to him, "Sir, give me

147

this water so that I won't get thirsty and have to keep coming here to draw water." He told her, "Go, call your husband and come back." "I have no husband," she replied. Jesus said to her, "You are right when you say you have no husband. The fact is, you have had five husbands, and the man you now have is not your husband. What you have just said is quite true." "Sir," the woman said, "I can see that you are a prophet. Our ancestors worshiped on this mountain, but you Jews claim that the place where we must worship is in Jerusalem." "Woman," Jesus replied, "believe me, a time is coming when you will worship the Father neither on this mountain nor in Jerusalem. You Samaritans worship what you do not know; we worship what we do know, for salvation is from the Jews. Yet a time is coming and has now come when the true worshipers will worship the Father in the Spirit and in truth, for they are the kind of worshipers the Father seeks. God is spirit, and his worshipers must worship in the Spirit and in truth." The woman said, "I know that Messiah" (called Christ) "is coming. When he comes, he will explain everything to us." Then Jesus declared, "I, the one speaking to you—I am he."

If I was living back then, the Samaritan woman and I would have been besties. She would not have been alone at that well because I would have joined her since I too walked in shame and believed I was an outcast so produced it quite well in my life. I can imagine us standing at the well discussing our issues we had with both men and woman, possibly blaming everyone else instead of looking inwards. The well would have been our place to vent and process through the unfortunate life we were living and how everyone hated us because we were just different, and they didn't like that. We would have left the well possibly feeling heard and validated, but not free. We would have continued in our day to day lives still living from a place of sadness, confusion, loneliness, brokenness and rejection; desiring to be loved but not understanding love itself and just how to get there. We would have looked forward to our time at the well mainly because it meant we were seen, heard, accepted and not judged for the way our lives turned out.

I also understand why her life was drastically changed forever when she met Jesus and drank from His living water. I too had my well moment which occurred in the one place I least expected, my bedroom. This was my moment where I experienced the real Jesus, not the one I was taught at home growing up or at church, but the one the Samaritan woman met as well. The beauty with my well moment is that it continues today to flow out into all areas of my life just like a ripple effect when a rock hits the water. That is the power of drinking from the living water of Jesus instead of a counterfeit version from man. One brings life eternal and one does not.

I experienced an awakening of my spirit when I drank from His water that day in 2012 that I will forever be grateful for. Even to this very day, Jesus continues to bring me back to that very moment so to show me a different perspective of His profound and All-circumferencing love and affection. There is so much power not only in His name and blood, but in the way He so beautifully and perfectly demonstrates love. His infinite and divine power continues to flow out and impact every area because of the magnitude of His Omni-potent presence. His word does not return to Him void so that means what He speaks out will come to completion and the substance within His word brings fullness not emptiness; produces life not death.

Isaiah 55:11NIV - So is my word that goes out from my mouth: It will not return to me empty but will accomplish what I desire and achieve the purpose for which I sent it.

There are zero side effects from the high I feel when I get filled and fueled with His presence and with His life shifting, altering, chain breaking and ground shaking kind of love. From the moment I met Him face to face, my life forever changed just like the Samaritan woman's did. There are no further writings after her well experience, but I can almost be certain that she became an example of the goodness and amazingly powerful love of Jesus to others in her community. I believe that they took notice of the change within her and began asking questions; wondering what was it that brought joy back into her step and a smile back on her face. For me, the impact of that moment at my own well with Jesus changed me forever, and I too am a living example of His transformational and life altering, agape love.

It was late in the afternoon on Good Friday, April 6, 2012 and I found myself in yet another relationship conundrum that brought with it those familiar feelings of anger, being a letdown, heartache, fear, rejection and uncertainty. The anger said, "What do you expect and how stupid can you be? The letdown said, "There you go again letting down God." The heartache said, "I can't take this anymore!" The fear said, "What are you going to do now? Will you ever love again? "Can I make it without him?" The rejection said, "You are not good enough for him and he figured that out and probably has found himself someone better." And finally, uncertainty said, "Are you sure you are doing the right thing here? Maybe you should go back and let him know you will do whatever he wants."

This familiar outcome I was now dealing with and processing through all began 2-1/2 years earlier when I chose to go against my gut and advice from a few Christian girlfriends and began dating a client of mine who I was extremely attracted to physically, but who I knew was not right for me for a few reasons 1. He first asked me out when he was still married about 6 months earlier and I told him "NO!" 2. I had recently gone to a Tres Diaz retreat so was in pursuit of God again and feeling hopeful. And 3. I was dating a good Christian man who respected me, told me he loved me and did not need sex from me which also was a first and I welcomed that change.

My client was persistent and ruggedly handsome and there was this chemistry we had that was undeniable, but I stuck to my 'No,' sensing that nothing good could come from dating him especially since he was not even divorced yet. I still continued to see him as a client and even when he did separate from his wife of 20 years, I stuck with my 'No' and told him that once he was divorced legally, I would consider going out with him, but not sooner and that was only if I was available, which at the moment I was not.

Unfortunately, Christian guy pulled the wool over my eyes and decided to put the brakes on, stopped calling and texting and eventually sent me an email telling me he was not ready for a serious relationship. I believe steam came out of my ears after I read that email. I was so angry, and I felt more used by him than I did the ones I slept with after meeting them for the first time at a club. At least I knew where I stood with them and vice versa. This guy, the Christian played with my heart by talking about marriage and filling my head with all sorts of future possibilities of our life together and then sent me an email!! Rejection is rejection and I was so over it! Here I am going on retreats and doing what I thought was best by dating a Christian guy and not having sex and I was still getting rejected, used and taken advantage of? As I re-read his email, I said out loud and with anger something I continued to say throughout my life; "See! It just does not pay to be good!

As I was fuming over the recent email from Christian guy, another email came through and it was from ruggedly handsome guy. My insides flipped and my heart skipped a beat as I read a sweet email he sent me where he even shared the Rascal Flatts music video from his song, "Bless the broken road" and said He believed this was about the two of us. So, the man knows how to play, and I didn't care because it was exactly what I needed to hear and feel at that moment. And just like that, I quickly forgot about Christian guy. Oh, how I loved that feeling of butterflies flipping around in my stomach and so I decided to meet him for coffee, figuring what harm is in that? He knows where I stand with being just friends and coffee is safe.

Even though I had my Christian girlfriends advising me not to get involved with ruggedly handsome guy, I still decided to go and of course, made sure I looked super cute. I was highly attracted to this man and our chemistry was magnetic and the sparks were flying all over the place before I even took my first sip of coffee. At one point while we were sitting there, he slowly placed his hand on my thigh, and I think time stopped. I knew at that very moment what I wanted and that was to have sex with him, and all other rational thinking left along with my desire to please God and do the right thing.

It did not take long before we were making out in between sips. I had not experienced this type of attraction since my first Prince so the teenage girl within me so wanted to believe that maybe just maybe this was my 2nd chance at love and allowing me another shot at my happy ending. Before we parted ways, he passionately kissed me goodbye at my car and I honestly felt drunk and was dizzy after our lips parted. My imagination took it from there and I began playing out the movie reel in my mind looking forward to the next time I would get to see him and what I hoped eventually would take place between us.

Our 2nd date was off the charts! We had a nice and intimate dinner and I felt like I was on cloud 9. Our conversation was effortless, and I was intoxicated by the feeling raging within me; just with a look, touch or gentle kiss on my lips. I honestly was experiencing my breath being taken away like I had read about in some of those harlequin novels. Was this it? Was this the love they were talking about? We closed the restaurant and decided to continue our date inside his parked truck where we steamed up the windows with more than just talking. I loved every minute of it; kissing, talking, laughing and sharing dreams we had with each other. I felt like I was back with my Prince when we first began dating. I believed it to be the perfect date and I left there in time to run home, shower and head to work.

Before the weekend was over, the scenario I saw played out in my mind when we left the coffee shop came to life and it was way better than I had envisioned. I let go of all my past concerns and what once troubled me about him and began believing we were the perfect match and before Monday even came, I was 100% head over heels and Christian guy was definitely a thing of the past. Christian guy who?

At first, I loved doing life alongside him, he was outgoing, fun and exciting and introduced me to a life of weekend excursions, motorcycle racing, adventurist travels and passion that I never had experienced before. I continued enjoying all the excitement and how worldly he was and this for the most part helped me forget about his marital status. He continued to promise me that he was going to go see a lawyer and start divorce proceedings, but that never seemed to happen and as time went by and the excitement and newness wore off and reality stepped in, my conscious seemed to begin waking up along with the familiar voices within my head reminding me of what a bad and sinful person I am.

Through all of this, I was still attending church and to my delight he began coming with me. I then began justifying our relationship as something God arranged because he was going to church now, like the sin isn't a sin if we attend church together? Whatever would help ease my guilt, I tried my hardest to believe, so I felt better about my sin. As we passed our 1st year anniversary things inside me became more confused and troubled and not as easy to ignore. One minute I was okay with my predicament because of how much I loved him and the next knew it was not right and things needed to change.

I was used to wearing masks, but this was harder than I thought to pull off. Here I was worshipping in church, listening to the sermons, reading the bible and deep down knew I was a complete fraud and a hypocrite. Once again, it was not hard to find people that thought there was nothing wrong with our relationship situation, so I made sure to talk to them and avoided my Christian girlfriends that spoke truth and did not water down God's word. Deep down I knew what I was doing was not right in the eyes of God and I just could not shake that no matter how much I tried.

Just like all my other relationships, I morphed into what he wanted me to be, changed my personality, the way I dressed, (he liked me to dress with less), passionately went after all his hobbies, rooted for his favorite football team and became his biggest fan hoping all along that he would do as he promised; file for divorce and pick me. As the 2-year mark approached and still nothing had changed with his relationship status; my restlessness increased, as did my battle within and I was being consumed with this debate going on within my head.

During this internal struggle, I decided to join a small group with my church, and this was the best decision I had made in a long time. For the first time, I began slowly letting some of my walls down and allowed these wise women in. After a couple of months of meeting, I felt safe enough to share with them my situation and they surprised me because they did not judge me, they just listened and loved me. One of these wise women said to me... "You are enough!" That's it, no explanation, just those three words. I was a bit confused at the time as to what she meant, but something inside wanted to desperately believe her and the confidence and sincerity in her voice resonated deep within. That time in that small group ignited something within me and led me on a new pathway in pursuit of God on a deeper level and brought about a desire to get to know the grace-filled God they all knew and were talking about. It allowed a door to open that at the time I was unaware of but the seed she planted began to grow and grow at a rapid pace.

As I began trusting and partnering with more of Gods truth about me and about Him and as I began opening more of my heart to Him as well, my love grew for God, but the pain within me did too. This pain was something I was not familiar with because it had nothing to do with my earthly relationships, but just my heavenly one. I did not want to disappoint God anymore but not due to guilt or shame or any other religious beliefs but because I began experiencing a glimpse of God as my dad not as a disciplinarian and so wanted to honor, respect and obey Him but from a place of love not duty. It's like I grew a conscious suddenly and this conscious was making up for the years it had been silenced.

I knew deep down that I could not keep living this type of lifestyle when I knew God did not approve and I began desiring his approval for a change. The battle within raged and every week during and after church I would weep knowing that I could not keep living this way. Yet the fear of losing my guy and what I believed was a future with him outweighed the pull to fully surrender myself and my selfish ways over completely to God and so this tug of war continued to play out week after week.

I was getting very good at negotiating skills and continued making plea bargains with God, this time praying for Him to show my guy that he needed to do what was right by me, divorce his wife and marry me. Please pick up my glass slipper and chase after me! Pick me! Pick me! As I found myself once again in pain, pouring out my heart to God, explaining my needs and pleading with Him to fix and change my guy, do my will and make the pain go away; He answered but not the way I was hoping. He brought a memory back of the time in my bedroom when I was flipping through all the pages of my journals and lightbulbs started going off. Good Grief! I'm at it again, nothing has changed has it? And just like that, things came into view and I did not like what I was seeing.

I sat there understanding what God wanted me to do, but at the same time, I knew I was still not ready to end things completely and so I instead presented my terms to God, which was to stop having sex with my guy, we could sleep in the same bed when he visited on the weekends but that's it. This seemed reasonable to me and helped ease some of the turmoil brewing inside, so I thought. Well, the inner battle did not let up even with us not having sex anymore because the fact was in Gods eyes, my guy was still married, and I was interfering with a special covenant of His. The reality of what the underlying issue and truth was just brought about more discomfort knowing that additional change was still necessary. I still can't Lord, I still can't. I love him and I can't imagine doing life without him. Help me please! I still had the pain of knowing I was living this lie and I knew God did not approve and in addition a new pain joined in when my guy quickly began retreating by calling me less and would decide to not come see me on the weekends as much.

My heart was hurting so badly, and I just could not get any rest or peace within. Soon, he was only calling me about every 5th day which was the opposite of what he used to do. He went from calling or texting me several times a day to possibly calling me once the entire week. He would end the call with I love you and that still brought me hope, but his actions brought confusion and fear. When I asked him why he was not calling, he would tell me that I was being insecure and convince me that nothing was wrong, and I was the one with the problem. I would hang up feeling guilty and like I had done something wrong or expected too much of him to call me more than once a week. I would ridicule and shame myself and begin the self-talk necessary to help me work through and deal with my feelings. I even went to a few co-dependent group meetings to find out if he was right.

Since my dad was no longer living and was the one I normally went to for guy advice, I instead decided to call a good guy friend of mine that I could always count on to be upfront and honest with me and shared with him what was transpiring and that I wanted his guy perspective because he was in a relationship and I trusted him. He told me that he calls his girlfriend daily because he wants to hear her voice and that what my guy was doing was not right and that I was not asking too much. I knew deep down that he was right, and this just brought more pain knowing that I was in fact losing him.

About two weeks went by and nothing had changed on the Homefront, including my feelings of confusion and uncertainty of where I stood with my guy. I continued to battle back and forth with guilt, shame and feelings of doing something wrong and my prayers now to God were more like pleas to help ease my pain and shed some additional light on this situation making it clear as to what I am to do, knowing full well that He had already made it clear but hoping His plan had changed.

I remembered a scripture verse my mom would always tell me to pray when you want discernment and I began including this scripture in my pleas to God as well. John 17:17 Consecrate me in truth Lord, your word is truth, keep me from being deceived! And within a couple of days, He answered and this time, I was willing to listen and willing to obey.

It was the week of Easter and my guy had left on another business trip to Tennessee and things began playing out just like all the other weeks. We had made plans to spend the weekend together but as Friday came, still no calls or texts from my guy. He had just told me the Sunday before that He loved me and even would consider marrying me because he never was loved so well by anyone else and he did not want things to end. I had believed him and yet, another 5 days had gone by and still no call and I sat there in the middle of my bedroom floor so confused, so exhausted with myself and this roller coaster ride I was yet again choosing to be on.

It was late Good Friday and I was so done with it all! I cried out to God in desperation to once again take this cup from me Lord because I just can't do this anymore! I have nothing left inside me to push through. I need you to help me; I'm used up and tired and I just want all this pain to go away! I'm so tired of being hurt; I'm so tired of not mattering to anyone! I'm so tired of not being good enough! I sank to the ground defeated, depleted and as I took a deep breath screamed out for mercy and help and something happened that changed my life forever.

As I was kneeling in the middle of my bedroom sobbing and crying out to God, I felt my room fill with a presence that took my breath away and overwhelmed me with a sense of love, acceptance and peace. His presence of love was so overwhelmingly powerful that I could hardly move. As I knelt there, I entered a vision for the very first time in my life and there He stood before me in the middle of my bedroom. His arms were stretched out as if He wanted to hold me, but I instead fell face down at His feet and cried my eyes out doing as Mary Magdalene did and wiping the tears that dripped on his feet away with my own hair.

I felt at that moment what Mary Magdalene must have felt, The Samaritan woman and the woman with the blood disorder all rolled into one. I knew in that instance why Mary never left His side. The beauty of that moment imprinted on my heart and every inch of my being became delivered and healed. I could feel the transformation taking place within my heart, spirit and soul and I knew as I experienced this encounter, that my life would forever be changed and for once I was no longer confused as His love washed over me. As I continued to weep, I heard Him clearly say ever so gently; "Baby girl, Give me your pain." He called me, Baby Girl!" I felt each endearing word awaken dead places within me and I knew it was necessary to listen and do as He asked.

I saw this huge black blob appear which I knew represented all the darkness I had allowed into my life over the years. It was bigger than me and I managed to somehow pick it up and hand it over to His welcoming arms. I watched as He took ahold of it with such ease, turned around and then exited the room. I fell back to the floor, on my knees and continued to weep, and I heard the audible voice of God say... "I need you to sacrifice the relationship once and for all." There was no question within me what He meant by that and this time I was ready and so through tears, shook my head, Yes in agreement and let Him know that when I saw my guy on Easter Sunday, I would end things. I couldn't' help but let out a little chuckle as I realized the significance in what He had just asked of me and what Good Friday represented in my Christian faith. Oh Lord, you have a sense of humor; I spoke out loud and chuckled some more through the tears.

I still felt a heavy sense of loss knowing that soon things would come to a complete close between my guy and I, but at the same time I felt joy bubbling up knowing that I will be okay because I was not doing it alone anymore. A sense of peace was birthed that night within me, and I could feel it as it washed over me starting at my head and flowing down to eventually cover my entire body. The heavy cloak of shame and unworthiness lifted off me and I felt lighter and like I said earlier, my confusion lifted as well.

There was this feeling of safety, significance, value and worth that erupted within me that I had never felt before and I welcomed them all. I knew that everything would be different from this day forward in my Christian walk and I was okay with that. As I handed over to Him the pain of my past, He replaced it with a fire deep within me to want more of Him and Him alone. I knew that I would never ever straddle the fence again and that I was now a new creation through and through. I heard those sweet words spoken out by my bible study leader that day to me; "You are enough!" but this time, it made sense to me and I understood and accepted myself worthy as His beloved, His Daughter, His bride and that Jesus wanted me to Himself and I too desired that and it felt good.

As I continued sitting in the middle of my bedroom floor; crying mainly from a place of mourning the loss of the relationship; waves of His peace and hope continued to wash over me and I welcomed it knowing that a new day, a new season and a whole new journey was being established at that exact moment. And as the tears flowed, they soon shifted to tears of joy because for the first time, I saw myself valuable, worthy, loved, cherished and forgiven and it felt so good.

Cocoon Time

The encounter in my bedroom that day was intentional just like His encounter was at the well with the Samaritan woman. He showed me that moment something I never quite understood or felt worthy of—grace. He loved me despite my sinfulness. He did not see my sin, He saw me. He loved me in a way I had never been loved before. That day, like the Samaritan woman, I began receiving His living water instead of mans. This encounter was the beginning of my spiritual transformation. I began my dance of intimacy with Jesus and I have never stopped dancing.

John 4:13-14: - "Jesus answered, 'Everyone who drinks this water will be thirsty again, but whoever drinks the water I give them will never thirst. Indeed, the water I give them will become in them a spring of water welling up to eternal life."

When I took my cup of living water out of the hands of Jesus that day in my bedroom and chose to drink from it, I knew and felt that everything was going to be different from that moment forward. Something happened inside me that I find hard to explain but I just knew I was different and for the first time understood what the bible verse meant about being a new creation, the old is dead, the new is here. This scripture came to life within my room because Jesus is The Word made flesh so Jesus Himself pierced through my flesh and ignited my heart and spirit so that I too could live in perfect harmony with Him and no longer a slave to the ways of this world; believing I would find my peace, my significance and joy from man, an unreliable source of all three, when in fact my one true source of life is and will always be Jesus.

2 Corinthians 5: 17 - NIV Therefore, if anyone is in Christ, the new creation has come: The old has gone, the new is here!

That life altering encounter stirred, shifted and shook things within me; rearranged, readjusted, restored and redeemed me in ways I thought were impossible, but now I know with God, all is possible. God performed a miracle on my spirit, my heart and my soul at a time I was so desperate for Him and He came through. To this very day that special bonding moment I experienced with Jesus still brings tears of joy to me whenever I reflect on it. From the moment I managed to pick myself up off the floor and take a few steps out of my bedroom, I saw, felt and heard things differently. I knew I had a tough road ahead of me, but I felt hopeful, cared for and not alone. This was a whole new territory for me, yet it felt right, and it felt good. Even though, at that time I was yet again, dealing with regret and rejection, I had strength inside me that I had never had before. I knew that the decision I had made that day was right in the eyes of God and that was all that mattered to me. That alone was a miracle.

God imprinted on me that day in my time of distress. He declared me His and His alone and I have never been the same since. It is no different than when a human imprints on a struggling animal; that animal can no longer go into the wilderness and be wild. I too can no longer go back into the wild because God has declared me His and His alone. My wild life is a thing of the past and I will no longer be able to survive out in the wild. From that day forward, I knew I had His approval, acceptance and love and realized that was all I needed and what truly mattered. I began seeing myself differently because I now was looking to God to define me instead of man. For someone desiring so badly to be accepted, chosen, belong, and just fit in, this newfound mindset and heart transplant was life changing to say the least. Because of that, I am grateful to God every day for never giving up on me or forsaking me even when I was in my darkest hour.

As I daily continued to strengthen and nurture my spirit man with spiritual truth and nourishment, things began to quickly shift and change for me. God was making up for all the years I had been wandering in the desert; I had a lot of catching up to do and I was willing and eager to do whatever He desired of me. Scripture became a fuel source and nourishment for my spirit and soul and my prayers became a way of getting to know Him better as a friend not foe. Long gone were rehearsed or memorized prayers, pleas for help or demands for Him to change someone else to accommodate me. My prayers became more about worship and praise not about me or another person. I began talking one on one to my heavenly Dad, Jesus and Holy Spirit with a deep desire to know more about them. I was no longer bargaining, negotiating or manipulating them in prayers. Religion was a thing of the past and I soon was having discussions with them as if they were sitting down next to me and in many cases they were. I practiced this new art of communication with them; no longer bowing my head, closing my eyes or folding my hands but instead doing the opposite. Talking with them where and whenever I could, eyes and hands open ready and willing to receive all they had for me. It didn't matter where I was, I just wanted to be in conversation with them, absorbing as much knowledge as I could and understanding the truth of their hearts for me and others. There was truly an awakening within my spirit, and it showed in my day to day actions not only with how I dressed, my behavior and my treatment towards others, but my lifestyle choices as well. My mindset had drastically been transformed from slavery, victim and orphan to daughterhood. The old way of thinking was now dead, and I was learning for the first time how to think like a daughter of a King. This too changed so many areas of my life. I no longer looked upon things from a perspective of brokenness, but from His perspective, a new perspective of wholeness.

Everything in and around me began taking on transformation including my bedroom. What once was a place of sex, pain, shame, hopelessness, loneliness, rejection and regret, became a place of inner healing, worship, church, laughter, renewed hopes, dreams and wholeness. I love how God restores and makes all things new, improved and beautiful. I looked forward to the nights now when

I knew I would have a date with Jesus so we could sit down and deal with any lies I still believed so He could then replace it with His truth. This became my new and very welcomed dating life.

Philippians 4:13 - I can do all things through Christ who strengthens me.

Now almost 8 years later I can look back and see His hand in all of this; in the pain, the suffering, the traumas, the awakenings, the struggles, the battles and the victories. I see why He brought those women into my life at the exact moment He did, and why He pursued me with such vengeance because He was preparing my heart for the exact moment Jesus would meet me face to face in my bedroom. I can now see how He was aggressively and intentionally working behind the scenes to fulfill plans He had for me for today. I just needed to wake up and catch up and so I have, and I rejoice in it all.

I recently was listening to a podcast by Pastor Steven Furtick of Elevation Church and what he said resonated within me, and I knew I needed to go to my Father with it, so to go deeper. He said... "Judas was necessary for Jesus to get to the cross." Man! That is powerful! I had never thought about that before, but it makes total sense. I quickly readjusted my perspective of ruggedly handsome guy and thanked God for him since possibly he was my Judas. I had already been thanking God for him and asking him to bless him wherever he was, but this new perspective brought me to a whole new level of forgiveness and thanksgiving.

The next thing God said to me took me even deeper; He asked.... "Who have you been a Judas to?" Ouch; that one stung a little, but I got it and thanked Him for showing me another perspective which would bring about humility, not pride within me. How quickly I had jumped to pride thinking others were my Judas's and not look at myself first. Progress not perfection, Thank You Jesus! It is those sweet and intimate moments I have with God that I am so very grateful for that time at my well because It developed within me an ability to enter into a relationship with my Heavenly family that is genuine and from a place of humbleness knowing there is so much for me to learn and I know they are the ones I desire to glean from. I long for that and I am totally okay with God correcting me because it develops within me the character Jesus demonstrated here while walking this planet.

At first I believed that the encounter I experienced in my bedroom represented me breaking out of my cocoon of shame and slavery to sin, but as time has passed and I have gone deeper into transformational healing, the understanding of My Father's heart for me and for my healing; I have discovered that it was just the birthplace and beginning of my time inside my cocoon where the biggest transformation would take place. The encounter was the gateway for me to get on a new path, discontinue my journey around my mountain of shame and the life cycle I was on, choose to surrender all future outcomes to Jesus and no longer needing to control my outcomes due to fear.

Once the encounter was over and the relationship was sacrificed, Jesus slowly and gently began challenging me and getting me very uncomfortable. The first few months after my encounter were not easy. Yes, He so graciously healed me completely of all lust, perversion, fantasy, unworthiness, and my need to cope with a broken heart by running into the arms of other men, but I was still left with the original brokenness and pain which had led me down that path to begin with. I had to still look at myself in the mirror everyday fully aware of my past, all the bad choices I had made, all the people I had hurt and letdown, including myself. That's the thing about addictions; you hurt those that you love and there are side effects and consequences that you must deal with once you have decided to quit. In addition, I experienced betrayal and rejection all over again when I found out my guy had been in another relationship while we were still together. The difference and might I add huge sign of His redemptive glory and healing power is this time I had no desire to cope by running into the arms of another man but I instead, received comfort for my pain by running into the arms of Jesus, hugging tightly and never letting go.

During this rebirthing, reparenting, re-establishing, restoring, renewing, redirecting and realigning time in my cocoon, I had to learn new ways of thinking and processing and unlearn old ways of thinking and processing. I am continuing to learn how to love from God's perspective; how to receive love without feeling manipulated, trapped or fearful and I have had to relearn how to show love without manipulation, control or use it as a form of punishment. This new journey has required me to get very uncomfortable at times, more than I can count and relearn how to do every kind of relationship there is, so to start and stay on new pathways Jesus is establishing for me. I have had to learn why I became so uncomfortable with love in the first place and allow Jesus to help me repair those areas so I could become comfortable with His perfect love. I could go on and on because 30 years of slavery and self-punishment will have side effects and consequences.

I believe my moment of breaking free from my cocoon and allowing my wings to stretch out so I can fly will be when I leave this planet and see Jesus face to face. That will be a time where freedom will be taken to a whole new level and a whole new realm of existence. I rejoice today, knowing that this journey I have been on and am still on is predestined by Him and I too am passionately pursuing His heart for me with freedom as my goal. Regardless of it all, I welcome the change, I welcome the struggles so to change, and I welcome his sweet corrections and I am forever grateful and like James, consider and count it all joy.

James 1:2 - "Consider it pure joy, my brothers and sisters, whenever you face trials of many kinds because you know the testing of your faith produces perseverance. Let perseverance finish its work so that you may be mature and complete, not lacking anything."

I must admit there are times I have discussed with my heavenly Dad why He didn't just make everything brand new that day. Why did He just heal me of the lust and the need for men's attention? Not that I am ungrateful for that part because I have never been tempted since, but why not the whole enchilada? Even though I did ask this question of Him, I pretty much already knew the answer before He spoke back. He loves perfectly well and that means not being an enabler and fixing everything for me. He is not Co-Dependent, so He desired to empower me and equip me by allowing me to walk through this relearning, rediscovering and growing process I have been on as a result of my past mistakes and shortcomings.

It is through these times of inner challenges that I have persevered which led me to grow in wisdom, knowledge and strength. I had to walk this inner transformational healing journey out so I could then be used by God to help others on theirs. I have had to earn my time in the arena that I chose to fight in and from. I have gained knowledge, understanding, strength, counsel, might and wisdom walking hand in hand with Jesus while discovering new ways to connect and love again like He so beautifully and perfectly does. Jesus, God and Holy Spirit have loved me well so I too can learn to love others well. It is a journey of rediscovery and restoration that I consider necessary and one I am forever grateful for. Today, I see everything from a different perspective, and it is due to this time in my cocoon. I no longer see the triggers and promptings from Holy Spirit as any type of annoyance or inconvenience but instead as signs of just how much God loves me because He desires additional healing for me more than I even do and I welcome them all with heartfelt thanks.

My love of Suddenly

Encounter: Take Two

Our God is a God of continuous pouring out, limitless possibilities, perfect timing and super-duper *suddenly's*. I am a big fan of His *suddenly's*. His *suddenly* moments produce life altering outcomes to say the least. The 1st time I experienced a suddenly was the encounter and the next time was about 2 years later. I was going about my day, minding my own business and out of nowhere, I heard Holy Spirit whisper ever so gently in my ear... *"Baby Girl, I need you to go back to the encounter because I have something new to show you."* As He whispered in my ear, I could feel His presence all over me like I had in my bedroom that day 2 years earlier. He literally startled me when I first heard His gentle voice and then immediately as His presence grew, I became submerge within the vision and I began to weep with what I saw being played out. I was feeling everything within my inner core as I watched the vision play out before my eyes. I had never thought about going back and getting a different perspective, but Ummm? God did. He's just so smart like that. How sweet of God to desire for me to see this new and improved perspective and knew the perfect time that I would be ready to see it. Many things stayed the same, but one thing changed because I was no longer living in or from shame and God knew that. This is what I saw:

- I was on my knees crying out to God.
- Jesus walked in with His arms wide open.
- I remained at His feet crying, wiping his feet with my hair.
- He asked me to give Him my pain and sin.
- I handed Him the big black blob.
- He took it from me and left the room. (This is where I thought it ended). Well nope!
- He quickly placed it down and ran back, knelt beside me and wrapped me up in His arms. (Still chokes me up, and I can still feel the intensity of the moment as I write). Thank you for that, Jesus.

Oh, my goodness! He did not leave me alone there to cry and mourn through the pain of loss and rejection. He did not abandon me when I needed Him the most! He was not ashamed of me! He came back for me, took me in His arms and comforted me. He came back and He loved me. Well, to say I was not undone would be like saying Sheep don't Baaaa! What I love so much about this part of my journey is God's perfect timing, knowing the exact time I would be able to not only see this changed outcome, but receive and accept it too. This new perspective of my initial encounter brought along with it another upgrade of healing for me. It's like I was bumped from coach to 1st class without expecting it and what a nice and *sudden* surprise that always is. I also love how He transformed what I once feared in relationships; (surprise and sudden endings) and made it instead something to look forward to. He makes all things new!

Encounter: Take Three

This time, God decided to have some fun with me so pulled one of His *suddenly* moments while I was shopping at a nearby grocery store. I was once again minding my own business, going through the organic section and enjoying some quiet alone time. I slowly made my way from one aisle to the next and Wham! It felt like I walked into a wall and just like that, my wall transformed into one very large heavenly presence. I quickly regained my balance and just stood there next to the organic teas almost stunned with what just happened. I began sensing the overwhelming presence of His love and I could hardly keep my composure. I was leaking at my eyes and vibrating all over like the Duracell bunny on high doses of caffeine. I heard that sweet whisper again saying the same beautiful words. *"Baby Girl, I need you to go back to the encounter because I have something new to show you."* And then He softly added, *"I imprinted on you that day Baby Girl, I imprinted on your heart, you are mine."* Okay, that's it, I'm done! I knew this *suddenly* of His was very important so I just left my cart there in the middle of the aisle, put my shades on so no one could see all the tears streaming down my face and high-tailed it out of there. I jumped into the driver's seat of my car and burst into tears. Before I even managed to get all the way home and into my garage, the vision started coming and Wow, it sure had changed!

- I was on my knees crying out to God.
- Jesus walked in with His arms wide open. *"Stop right there."* He gently said to me.

This is what I saw play out which changed my entire perspective of Jesus and my understanding of just how precious, perfect, pure, unconditional and beautiful His love truly is.

The entire vision changed as I instead saw my beautiful friend, Jesus just go and take me into His arms, hold me close and love on me. He kept kissing me on my forehead while He had the sides of my face cupped in His mighty hands. I could see the markings on His wrists, right below the palms on both sides. I remember touching them at one point and just cried even harder knowing what He had gone through for me. This time, I received it as genuine love not punishment. He kept wiping my tears away and reassuring me of how much He loved me and how proud He was of me. I heard as He softly said…. *"Baby Girl, I did not come here because of your sin; I came to just love on you. I saw you not your sin."* I knew right then in that moment, sitting in my car inside my garage, tears streaming down my face that I was healed from all religious false beliefs and would no longer be held back by the fear and misconception it produced.

I have grown very fond of His *suddenly's* and I choose every day to submit to whatever level of encounter He chooses to engage me in. I know that there are so many mysteries about heaven, Jesus, God Himself, Holy Spirit and The Super Natural Realm and as I am no longer walking in fear of man or any religious views, I am able to step in and engage His presence in ways I have never done before that day. I have removed any limits I had placed on God, Jesus, Holy Spirit and myself and just trust in His goodness, faithfulness and perfect timing; sit back, buckle up and enjoy the ride.

I get out of bed every morning and say, Papa, I am all in! Use me, guide me, instruct me, show me your heart and teach me whatever you desire for me to learn today. I imagine His shepherds' hook and I grab ahold of the one end as He leads me around. I just know there is so much more for me to learn and I just cannot wait for another suddenly.

For me, the sky is not the limit when it comes to God because there is no limit with Him. I imagine myself as the little girl sitting on her swing set swinging as high as she can and I am not alone this time for my heavenly dad is gently pushing me from behind and knows when I am swinging high enough and when I need to slow down so not to fall off and hurt myself. He is a perfect Father I know I can trust, lean on and allow to guide me throughout life knowing He will always have my back and never leave me and if I am to fall, He will be there to pick me up, dust me off and kiss any boo boos I have and make them all better.

Come fly a little higher

Whatever path you have chosen to continue on, whatever mountain you are choosing to keep circling, I personally understand the agony of defeat when you believe you have won the battle to instead find yourself wandering around yet again. I know too well the feeling of shame, regret and fear that keeps you from moving forward because you believe you do not deserve anything better or maybe you just can't do it. I understand the confusion that sets in and you don't even know whether you are coming or going, or which way is up or down. I understand the battle that rages within and the anger that builds inside that at times you just want to scream, and you begin contemplating whether your life is even worth living.

I remember too well all the toxic thoughts swirling around in my head telling me that I deserve bad things in life, I don't matter or if

I died no one would even care. I have lived through high levels of anxiety where I even considered slitting my wrists because maybe then my pain would be gone. I know what heartache feels like on so many levels and I know what disappointment feels like too. *I get it that sometimes it just seems safer and easier to settle for the struggle than struggle when you don't settle.*

And then God blessed me with His gift of suddenly, that allowed me to meet the real Jesus and discover how beautiful and perfect His love is and the resurrecting power He represents. I now am living proof of just how transformational His love is and will always be. His love is a love that transcends all other types of love. It healed, resurrected and transformed many men and women written about in scripture and it continues to transform all who are willing to partake and drink from His cup of living water today.

His perfect love does not have geographical boundaries and shows no favoritism. He loves all His children regardless of their lifestyle choices. I mentioned this earlier and it is worth repeating; His word says in John 14:18 that *He will not leave us as orphans, He will come to us.* If He played favorites, it would read; I will come for a few of you that I have chosen, not all of you because I play favorites. Personally, that spoke volumes to my orphan self that needed reassurance that she was not forgotten, left out or abandoned. I also can say from experience that there was a huge difference in my outcomes when I completely surrendered myself and my lifestyle choice over to Jesus and allowed Him to lead me out of my darkness instead of trying to do it in my own strength. I now taste, see, experience and know the feeling of victory and joy *in Jesus, not man.* I'm here to tell you that it far outweighs any feelings of shame, fear, rejection and regret my previous lifestyle produced and is a free gift available for you too with no strings attached, no annual fees, contracts to sign or guilt trips if you stumble and fall or come up short.

I want to share and bless you with a dream I had one night about 4 years ago. In my dream I was standing with Jesus in the main room in our basement of the house I live in now. This room is quite large and there is a single small window on the outside wall. In this dream, Jesus pointed out the window to me and said; *"Sometimes, we are so focused on the doors that we miss out on the windows."*

Jesus is a man of little words but the words He speaks are profound and cover a lot of ground and I stood there completely aware of the message He was trying to teach me. *Blessings come to us in all shapes and sizes and if I am looking for big doors of opportunities, blessings and circumstantial turnaround, I will miss out on all the Window of opportunities and little ways He is blessing me and the importance of being aware of all His blessings no matter the size.*

He then directed my attention to the ceiling and small clear balloons were all drifting down above us. I noticed that inside each clear balloon was a beautiful small silver gift box with a silver ribbon on top. I turned to Jesus in excitement and noticed that He was holding a long needle in His hand and as my eyes caught sight of the needle, He extended it over to me, offering it to me but not forcing it upon me. I retrieved the needle with excitement and eagerly began popping each balloon to release the gifts that were held inside. I felt like a kid in a candy shop as I popped as many balloons as I could, laughing and receiving each gift as they fell from their original nesting place. He then spoke again and said; "Look how easy it is to receive My gifts." I once again understood exactly what He meant. *I had believed growing up that I had to work for the love, acceptance and approval of my parents and even then, it was not good enough and that mindset transferred over to my relationship with God, Jesus and Holy Spirit. I believed I had to work for their love, acceptance and approval too and Jesus was healing me of this mindset and false belief at a time I was asleep, resting and not working.* When I awoke in the morning, I knew something had taken place within my spirit and my soul, and I was super excited to enter into a whole new level of relationship with God, Jesus and Holy Spirit minus guilt or worry of not measuring up.

I am here today, a free woman; no longer led by sexually sin, perversion, lust, fantasy, orphan, slave or victim mindsets; to tell you that nothing and no one can fill a void in your life or complete you, but Jesus. I moseyed through life on an emotional roller coaster because I chose to place all my identity, worth and value in what others said or believed about me. I was looking for others to make me happy and that is not their job to do in the first place; that was a 'me' thing, something I had to figure out. Happiness is a choice and one I had to make regardless of my circumstances or relationship status. That is way too much pressure, power and responsibility to be placed on someone else's imperfect shoulders. It took me dying of me to see, accept and receive that truth so pride could take a back seat and allow Jesus to lead me to sanctification; clean and free from the pollutants of shame and disgrace.

I'm not trying to preach here or sound religious, just speaking truth from my own experiences in life which is all I can do. *The answer is always Jesus!* It is true when the bible says; **He is The Way, The Truth and The Life.** He was the answer to filling every void inside of me once and for all. If by chance, you have never been introduced to the perfect grace of Jesus, this is a better time than any. Jesus is real and alive, and He desires an intimate relationship with you. I am here to tell you that the moment I personally chose to completely surrender my life over to Him; my own choice and for no one else, was the moment I truly experienced freedom and began to live, not just survive or make do.

If you decide this is that time to take the leap of faith and surrender your life to Jesus; all of it, not a portion. First and foremost, Yay You!!!! And if you are not ready, that is okay too. Jesus is about grace not shame and He's not going anywhere and is not hard to find. He loves you and when the time is right, you can come back to this page if you like or not. The choice is always yours and I know firsthand that shame, fear and guilt do not initiate long term intimacy with Jesus.

For those of you that have already committed your life fully over to Jesus, I encourage you to stop and ask Holy Spirit; "Is there any part of me I am not aware of that I have not surrendered fully?" Physically? (Your mind, soul, spirit or body) Relationally? (children, spouse, boss, friends) Financially? (income, tithes). If there is an area, He shows you; if you choose, go ahead and release it into the welcoming arms of Jesus and step away. I have found that with my children, I saw myself slinging them over to Him, so they were too far out of reach for me to grab them back.

Wherever you are at this moment, relax and get comfortable. Take a moment and prepare your heart to receive by playing a song of worship you love or sing a hymn you know and just BE. Take a few cleansing breaths and feel the tension and stress of the day leave your body as you exhale. When you are ready; close your eyes and imagine your younger self dancing with Jesus. Place your right foot on His left and your left on His right and grab ahold of His mighty hands for balance. Rest and just give Him permission to lead you in this beautiful dance of intimacy. You do not need to do a thing and if you need to, remind yourself of that if at times, you naturally try to take control back from Him. Take in every detail of His face, His hands, feet, His smile, laughter, and His eyes! When you are ready, gaze into His eyes and say this simple prayer:

Jesus, I believe you are the son of God, the one true Savior who died for all my sins; present, past and future, because you love me so much. Today, I accept the sacrifice you made on the cross for me. I ask that you come into my heart, my soul, my spirit and make me brand new. Today Jesus I choose to follow you. Amen! (Continue to dance and receive His goodness)

I want to leave you with a little bit of heavenly wisdom Holy Spirit blessed me with shortly after I experienced my well encounter and my first dance of intimacy. He said that with God everything is simple, and the enemy is the one that complicates and confuses. He then said that God can be recognized in *'RE'* words and the devil, *'D'* words. This allowed me to quickly see for myself who was behind what I was feeling or experiencing so I could either welcome more or shut it down. I have included a list of both on the following page so you too can begin recognizing which hand you are eating from.

RE WORDS (God)

Renew Receive Restore Return Release Rest Recognize Revive Realign Remain Redeem Re-establish Remake Remember Resuscitate Rejoice Reposition Revalue Reclaim Reproduce Remolding Reprioritize Relinquish Repayment Remove Relax Rejuvenate Readjust Refresh Recover Replenish Resolution Resolve Rebuild Repurpose Reconstruct Rededicate Reshape Recreate Reappoint Reconfigure Recalculate Rediscover Relief Reconcile Rescue Revisit Recalibrate Reset Reinvent

D WORDS (Devil)

Delusion Deceit Deception Depression Denial Disease Disturbed Disgust Detachment Delinquent Detention Destroy Decapitate Damage Disobey Debt Destruction Desolate Detained Disappointment Disillusion Dirty Dingy Dumb Dangerous Delirious Detained Destroy Dead Death Delusion

7 SANCTIFIED AND SET FREE

"Love yourself enough to change."

---

*T*hroughout this chapter there will be an opportunity for you to get uncomfortable and challenge yourself if you choose. Why the challenges? They are necessary for change and growth to occur from within. There will also be Activations which sets in motion the inner transformational adjustments Jesus is blessing you with. I highly encourage you to enter both so you can receive the healing Jesus so desires you to receive.

"A comfort zone is a beautiful place, but nothing grows there." Unknown

"The only way to change, is to change."

"Comfort awaits on the other side of discomfort."

Step I. The Necessary Process of Elimination

I have come a long way due to the loving and welcoming arms of Jesus, Father God and Holy Spirit, and today I still welcome any additional refining work that is needed and necessary for further change within me to take place. Even to this day, I still get triggered from time to time with certain words, actions or facial expressions due to hidden pain not yet uncovered and dealt with and I am totally okay with that. Through the unconditional perfect love of God, the wisdom of Holy Spirit and the encouragement from Jesus, when I sense the trigger, instead of running for cover due to fear or an inner need to lash out, I instead pull up a seat and get down to business with them.

I recognize triggers now as His love gates for me to enter, if I choose, for additional inner healing and redemption. I embrace these opportunities to go deeper instead of reacting and running. I see it as an opportunity for growth instead of a remembrance of pain from past emotional trauma. I embrace it knowing that additional breakthrough is right around the corner and I get uncomfortable knowing that comfort awaits on the other side. As I sense a trigger rising from within; I will even at times say to God, "Awe, you love me so much that you want me to receive additional healing, Thank you." Now that is growth and a new creation perspective!

As God so graciously leads me down this new path of restoration, sanctification and transformation, He continually speaks these words to me; "Get uncomfortable for Jesus," so every day I wake up ready and willing to do just that. Let me tell you something, if I may? This level of comfort I am referencing, did not just happen overnight. It has taken years for me to reach the level of trust I am now at with God, Jesus and Holy Spirit and in addition, with those around me. I am His beloved daughter and He is remolding me into something new and improved every day. I on the other hand, needed to do my part which was to submit, be open, flexible and pliable so He could remold me as He always saw me in the first place—spotless, pure and beautiful. This entire transformation process has been just that, a process, my time in my cocoon.

There was a lot of debris that had to get out of the way for me to begin even seeing myself as He has always seen me. One of the biggest transformations that occurred within me was when I not only accepted but received the truth that God was the only one, I needed acceptance and approval from, no one and nothing else. This too was a process of elimination and took time since I had become very comfortable with many toxic mindsets of my past. As I came out of agreement with all facets of orphan, slave and victim mindsets; replaced them with truths straight from the Fathers heart, slowly I began believing what I was speaking out over myself. His truth began eating away at all my internal baggage I was carrying around and partnering with. His divine truth spoken out was beginning to fill in all the many cracks in my internal foundation. These first stages in my cocoon eventually lead to total freedom from all my inner bondage and false identity which before this, was established externally; my family, friends, men, neighbors, relationship status, appearance, success level, etc., everything but God.

Jesus is so perfect with His timing and so gentle with His approach and touch. He very slowly, lovingly, and gently began wooing and courting me and in turn, I slowly began trusting Him more and more as we spent additional time together and I began learning firsthand how sweet and kind He truly was. When He knew I was ready and no sooner; He began introducing me to His perfect Father and Holy Spirit too. He helped guide me into receiving a different revelation of who; Father God and Holy Spirit truly are and will always be. They do not change, we do.

One of the best decisions I have ever made besides joining a small group, was to give permission for Jesus to be my husband; court me, woo me and demonstrate to me the character traits of a gentlemen; Holy Spirit, to take on the role as my teacher and wise counsel; reteach, counsel and correct me when necessary, and Father God, the role of my dad; and speak true identity, value and worth into me. They each knew how to perfectly love and re-parent me back to spiritual and emotional health. They each became a safe place for me to rest my head on, be real with and freely share the deepest parts of my heart with, without condemnation or shame. Over time through this transformation, sanctification and restoration process, my heart was able to heal, and I was able to begin seeing love as a safe place and myself and others through His eyes not my own.

It did not take long after my first encounter for Jesus to start phase two of my restoration process. He gave me the grace to deal with my pain from the loss of the relationship and the betrayal, and then He got down to business. He is always patient and kind and so about a month after my well encounter, He began the second phase which involved not just cleaning out my inner closet, but my literal closet as well. Since my spiritual and physical mindsets had completely changed and I was no longer living from a place of lust and shame, I could sense and feel His presence and hear what He was asking of me and out of love, quickly obeyed. My desire and passion had drastically shifted from pleasing myself and man to pleasing God.

I remember as Jesus very lovingly and gently nudged me to go into my closet and I did. As I entered my closet, I just knew what He wanted me to do; I sensed it deep within my spirit. This time though was different because I was not feeling ashamed but loved. He began showing me which clothes were now inappropriate for His beloved daughter to wear and I for a change agreed so humbled myself and willingly obeyed by removing those clothes. He said to me that I was going to start dressing for Him and Him alone and I honestly loved hearing that.

I was unaware at the time, but He was teaching me the dance of intimacy and trust that I shared with you in chapter 6. He then led me to the toys I owned and used for sexual pleasure and out they went too. Each day, He lovingly led me to something different and I would grab His hand and do as He asked filled with grace not shame. As I obeyed Him more breakthrough, healing and clarity came. I never felt like I was losing anything because I had already gained so much spiritually and emotionally. I was just so humbled by the amount of grace and love He was bestowing upon me each day. God is a God that always trades up, and as I willingly obeyed Him, He in turn blessed me abundantly.

This process of cleaning out my closet was transformational and healing. I was literally getting rid of my baggage and it felt good. It was closure on a dark part of my life, or should I say clothesure. Ha! Ha! God is patient and perfect in His timing and He knew just what I was ready for and when. Once I was done with my clothes, sex toys, and hooker shoes, (I'm a lover of shoes so a bit of toddler stubbornness resonated). He then explained about what I was allowing myself to watch and read and how that would affect my brain which then contaminates my heart and the decisions I make. Our eyes and ears are gateways to our heart, spirit and soul.

Luke 11:34-26 - Your eye is the lamp of your body. When your eyes are healthy, your whole body also is full of light. But when they are unhealthy your body also is full of darkness. See to it, then, that the light within you is not darkness. Therefore, if your whole body is full of light, and no part of it dark, it will be just as full of light as when a lamp shines its light on you."

I first began grabbing any pornography videos or playgirls I owned and tossed them out and figured that was it; Wrong! He explained the sneakiness of the enemy and how even certain fantasy novels, television shows and movies that glorify sex can lead us to sin. I had just spent over $200.00 on all 6 seasons of Sex and the City and their movies and He said get rid of it all. At first, I considered giving them to someone I knew so began negotiating with Jesus for just a second but could feel that He meant business so out it all went. After SNC DVDs, came any fantasy books I had purchased. I have to say, the entire elimination process was uplifting, freeing and liberating. Knowing that God was for me, not against me or ashamed of me and is very much alive and living within me made this process so much easier. I knew I was not alone anymore and that felt good. As I rid myself of my old garments of shame, regret and fear, Jesus replaced them with new garments of purity, beauty, grace and peace from His closet in heaven and this to me was the definition of being born again. I was now a new creation and it felt so good to finally recognize and accept that as truth.

2 Corinthians 5:17 –Therefore, if anyone is in Christ, the new creation has come: The old has gone; the new is here.

Challenge #1:

If by chance you too have been wearing any of the following clothes, maybe it's time to exchange them for an upgrade! Begin by inviting the presence of Holy Spirit in, He loves to be invited and then ask Him to show you where you need a fashion upgrade.

Holy Spirit, I invite and welcome you in as my counselor, teacher, comforter and friend. Will you please release upon my heart what your desires are for me regarding any tattered clothing I am still choosing to wear?

Clothes of:

- Shame
- Guilt
- Rejection
- Unworthiness
- Loneliness
- Confusion
- Poverty
- Regret
- Not belonging or good enough
- Victim
- Insignificance
- Failure
- Anger
- Sadness
- Abandoned/Rejected/Not wanted

Activation:

After Holy Spirit has highlighted any tattered clothes you need to replace; visualize yourself with Jesus throwing those tattered, old clothes away and trying on your new garments from His closet of freedom, acceptance, value and worth.

As You hand over to Jesus an old and tattered item of clothing, ask Him what the new garment He is replacing it with represents. Write this down. Do this with each clothing exchange. Once you have received each new garment from Jesus, take time to visualize yourself putting them on and imagine how it feels, take it all in and thank Him for the upgrade.

Proverbs 31:25 – She is clothed with strength and dignity, and she laughs without fear of the future.

Example: I handed a very tattered and worn item of clothing that represented shame and He replaced it with a beautiful garment of purity.

End this session with the following prayer:

Thank you, Jesus for your ability to calm my seas, your healing presence and your forgiving arms of grace and acceptance. Thank you for this opportunity of redemption and restoration of my brain, heart, spirit and soul. Jesus, as you wash away these areas within my brain that accepted lies as truth about myself and others and the areas of my heart and spirit that are scattered, wounded, broken and bleeding; begin repairing and restoring me by filling me back up with your truths straight from The Father's heart to mine. Begin showing me how you see me and the words you speak out about me. Jesus, cleanse and anoint my thoughts, purify my heart and anoint my spirit with truth. In your powerful and beautiful name, Amen!

Proverbs 3:5-6 – "Trust in the Lord with all your heart and lean not on your own understanding; in all your ways submit to Him, and He will make your paths straight."

Challenge #2

Below are a few truth-revealing questions to ask yourself and Holy Spirit when and if you become triggered or find yourself easily offended, hurt or repeating certain arguments with loved ones. It is when we are in relationships that the areas we still need healing in will emerge. (We get rubbed the wrong way, feel like we are being picked at; etc. etc.) Basically, you have something within you that has not been dealt with and it can feel like your spouse or friend is picking at it like a scab). Remember, forgiveness is for you, and for you to receive freedom, you will need to examine yourself, not others. *Example of a trigger: When I was a little girl, I struggled in math and my dad would try a help me with my math homework. He would become easily frustrated with me when I did not understand and vocalize his frustration. To this day, if I ask a question of my husband and he sounds frustrated with me, I immediately react and vocally disapprove of his response. This does not mean that he was frustrated by any means, it was the tone I heard, and it reminded me of my dad and so I reacted.* My wound, my trigger, my opportunity to love myself well by forgiving and releasing.

- What is the condition of my heart? (Examine it and be honest; is there undealt with bitterness, anger, shame, insecurity, fear, jealousy, vengeance?) If you find yourself angry a lot, fear is always the root.

- Is this my cycle playing out again? (Something you get triggered by repeatedly, familiar outcomes.)
- What comes out of my mouth when triggered? How do I respond? (What age do you sound and feel like?)
- Who(m) do I need to forgive and release judgment of in order to improve my heart condition and discontinue the triggers so to move on? (Who am I still freely giving my power over to?)
- When I am triggered, who does the person remind me of? (When there is unforgiveness in our heart, typically the person triggering you will have a trait the person that wounded you had.)

What has worked for my husband and I on this journey is that we sat down and listed out the triggers we are now aware of so we can recognize when one or the other is becoming triggered and support and encourage each other to go after additional healing. We also try not to trigger each other and if we do, we quickly apologize. We have learned to see it as the gateway for growth, maturity and emotional wholeness and we choose to love ourselves through this wholeness process by being vulnerable with each other too. The goal is always connection.

Bible Fact:

The word "Forgiveness" is mentioned in the NIV bible exactly 14 times, once in the Old Testament and 13 times in the New Testament. The word "Forgive" appears 42 times in the Old Testament and 33 times in the New Testament. The word "Forgiven" appears 17 times in the Old Testament and 28 times in the New Testament. And the word "Forgiving" appears 6 times in the Old Testament and 1 time in the New. Based on those findings I would conclude that forgiveness is important to God because He is love and has nothing to do with punishment. Unforgiveness is a form of punishment.

As more of myself died and as I continued practicing and demonstrating forgiveness instead of punishment; humility instead of pride and grace instead of legalism, I was able to not only see and hear His truth but receive it as well without feeling ashamed, but instead loved by a God who demonstrates it perfectly. I recognized and accepted the fact that I was the common denominator and that many of the things that were happening in my life were patterns and cycles of mine not the other persons. This revelation from the loving heart of my Father opened the floodgates of heaven for the glory of God to be revealed within my heart and my life. As I gave Him complete access into my heart, spirit and life by opening the doors of humility and grace, I was also giving Him permission to begin what He does best; restore, redeem, purify and sanctify. He slowly and ever so gently began a transformation process of my heart, spirit and soul that He continues to do even today. He began putting the pieces of my fragmented and scattered heart and soul back together.

As time passed, and I continued the process of eliminating toxic wounds and mindsets and took on a posture of openness and willingness to receive His more; that is exactly what began happening. I began receiving more healing, more redemption, more restoration, more sanctification, more grace, more wisdom, and more knowledge and so on and so on. God is a God of limitless possibilities and more than enough to go around. The outcome, and there is always one when we allow God to take care of our yukiness within, is eventually my unhealed wounds stopped calling the shots and my spirit grew stronger which produced different outcomes in my life. Different seeds were planted so therefore I began harvesting different fruit.

"Until, you become humble and vulnerable before Jesus and admit to the truth, you will stay blinded and imprisoned by the lie." M.A.

Bible Fact: *The concept of humility – Based on the King James version: The word humility is mentioned 7 times. The words humble and humbled are mentioned 56 times.*

Pathway to the heart

I'm not sure how many of you know anything about gardening and the importance of the soil? My own dad grew up on a farm and so he was an expert when it came to cultivating fescue in our yard. He knew the

right time to aerate, fertilize, lime, weed and seed. He had it down to a science and to this day, I do too. As a little girl, I learned from my dad, the

Matthew 15:18: But the things that come out of a person's mouth come from the heart, and these defile them.

importance of when to throw the seed or fertilizer and when not to. The soil had to be prepared and even tested at times. I also learned that you never threw fertilizer at the same time you seeded, or it would burn the seed up. These were great gardening tools my dad learned from his dad when he was a boy and was able to pass on down to me.

God too teaches me; His little girl similarly as my own dad did by using the teachings of my earthly dad and applying His word to it. For example, the above scripture verse regarding the condition of our hearts; He showed me the importance of allowing Him to come into my heart to begin preparing the soil so I would be able to receive His living word. It was a process but one necessary so when He began planting new and improved seeds, my heart was ready and able to receive, not reject them.

Before God could even begin plowing the soil of my heart, He had to first remove the huge wall of thorns I had erected to keep everyone out and that included God. Do you remember the fairytale Sleeping Beauty? Can you see the scene where the Prince rides up and there before him stood hundreds of huge thorny trees completely engulfing the castle? Inside, Sleeping Beauty sleeps and can only be awakened from loves first kiss. I say all of this because that too is exactly what Jesus is up against when we surround our hearts with walls of resentment, anger, bitterness, shame and rejection. We unknowingly erect those same thorny trees as barriers to keep everyone out and that includes Jesus, The Prince of peace. I had erected a huge barrier around mine in hopes of never getting hurt again. Thank goodness God is relentless in His pursuit of us and way more powerful than a fire breathing dragon, the devil himself. He quickly and intentionally went about removing my barrier by wooing me and showing me that He could be trusted. The more I listened to His sweet whispers of reassurance and truth, the more of my walls came down so He was then able to have complete access into the soil of my heart.

Since I had spent so many years choosing to cultivate lust, denial, shame, self-condemnation, pain and unforgiveness; the condition of the soil of my heart was dry, hard and cracked and in need of some serious repair. In addition, what my soil produced was not in any sense a lush carpet of healthy green grass or beautiful fragrant flowers, but instead a field of all sorts of unruly weeds that had taken over and had to be dealt with first. These weeds resembled all the fear, anger and pain I had allowed to consume my heart and the process of pulling them up required getting to the root below the surface and then replacing it with His truth. He was the perfect gardener of my heart, knowing the perfect times to weed and feed. He knew that for any new pathway to be established in my life, some serious soil renovation would be necessary.

As God's masterful gardening hand continued to plow and till away at the soil of my heart, it became softer and He was able to dig deeper so began removing tattered bitter roots and vines that had spread throughout. He then began the refill process by filling the empty gaping holes back up with His healthy soil and fertilizer straight from heaven to bring life back where it had once been dead, hard and cracked. The next stage was to plant His truths back in and nourish these truths with His living water straight from His throne of grace and mercy. This process was a necessary requirement if I wanted to form new anointed and divine pathways of freedom and end the pathways, I had been traveling for 30 years.

To this day He is still pruning me at times, and it can be quite uncomfortable and even hurt, but it too is necessary just like pruning our own bushes or trees in our yard, both produce healthier blossoms. As new seasons develop so do additional pruning, tilling, digging and seeding and not necessarily in any set order, but I have confidence in my heavenly gardener that He knows best, so I trust Him in the process. Through this soil rejuvenating process, supernatural change took place within my spirit and soul because I began choosing to take a chance on myself and gave permission to God to go after my inner hidden pain.

I saw my heart as a piece of clay and allowed God to be my potter and shape me into the finished work of art He always saw me as. It truly has been like this beautiful dance of intimacy between the two of us and one I will always treasure and look forward to. As I learned from my beloved creator how to love myself well, I began allowing the toddler, little girl, adolescent and young adult within me to be heard, encouraged and I in turn loved on her; and as I chose to forgive those that I believed hurt me, I was then able to fill those now empty voids in my heart, spirit and soul with His life giving truth.

During these many seasons of deep inner transformational healing, I had to be very intentional about coming out of agreement with things that were said or done to me as a little child and teenager and come into agreement with the truth spoken out to me by my heavenly Dad. It was through this practice of being intentional with my inner healing and what I was allowing myself to hold onto that developed within me new pathways of truth and knowledge of heavenly perspective verses earthly. I chose to see things differently which then lead me to living out life differently. I no longer looked to my past to define me because I began receiving my value, worth and significance that I never received as a child now from my heavenly dad who created me in the first place. I began allowing His grace to flow over and through me and His grace began ever so gently loving my heart, spirit and soul back to life.

This part of the healing process took several years and was quite draining for me due to my need to avoid and protect. It was way easier for me to duck and cover than face the truth head on which is what God desired me to do. Even allowing and accepting this process was a huge challenge for me because I lived more from a place of survival; shutting down and shutting everyone out so to feel safe. I had practiced keeping everyone at a distance so to finally take some ownership, humble myself and accept His hand to help me walk this out was a huge step toward inner healing and wholeness. I had become quite skilled at self-protecting, so typically warm feelings were kept at bay, shutting down emotionally when someone challenged me in that area especially if they did not seem safe. For God to penetrate my heart was a miracle. He had His work cut out for Him because in addition to the barrier of thorny trees surrounding my heart, was also a moat filled with great white sharks. Jesus is a shark whisperer too and my hero!

2 Chronicles 7:14- If my people, who are called by my name, will humble themselves and pray and seek my face and turn from their wicked ways, then I will hear from heaven, and I will forgive their sin and will heal their land.

Step II. New Perspectives

Perspective of God

Just think about this for a second…. Everything we believe about God is typically demonstrated and taught to us by our own parents since they are our first teachers. Have you ever stopped long enough to question that?

"Foggy lenses produce foggy images."

Marcia Ann Congdon

Have you ever stopped long enough and asked why you believe what you believe? Who says what they taught us about God was even true? It was from their own perspective which was taught to them by someone else's perspective and so on and so on. I hope you can see what I am trying to get at. I'm not judging all parents here or religious groups or saying what they taught us about God was wrong. What I am trying to point out here is to think about perspectives and just how you came to believe what you believe about God, Jesus and Holy Spirit. Each perspective was based on what lens and filter that person was looking through and from. Here are a couple of examples:

• If a person is raised in fear, and God is used as a tool to control? Guess what they might believe about God? Possibly, He is scary, controlling and not someone you want to get to know or have a relationship with. You most likely will grow up fearing Him and keep your distance, due to intimidation. Or you will obey and follow all the rules but not be able to engage and be in relationship with Him.

• If God is demonstrated to you by a parent or religious group as being very disappointed in you because you are a sinner and He wants nothing to do with sinners; well you as a child might grow up possibly believing that God is very judgmental, angry and has this ginormous measuring stick He keeps right beside Him and you just will never measure up in His eyes, so why even try. If the child always feels like a disappointment to their own parents, they will believe they are a disappointment to God too. They too will fear God and be a doer of His word, working hard to not disappoint God so therefore never resting in His love and just BE in relationship with Him.

• What if a child has demonstrated to him/her that God is very busy dealing with so many other things way more important than you? His plate is full and just does not have the time for you. This child might grow up possibly believing that they are invisible to God, not good enough, God is too busy dealing with children worthier than them and so is unavailable and not interested in hearing their needs. If they felt neglected emotionally by their parents, they feel neglected emotionally by God.

All the above examples I have not only processed through myself but have helped many others do the same. I have listened to countless clients openly share these perspectives of God, Jesus and Holy Spirit due to what was demonstrated in their own home and church environment when they were growing up. My continual advice is and will always be to get a different perspective; God's Jesus's and Holy Sprit's themselves and put aside what they once were taught by their own parents or someone else. We choose to love and forgive our parents because they are imperfect humans just like we are and then we go to the one who is perfect and is truth; Jesus. We lay down at His feet the lies we once believed which held us out of connection with Him and we open ourselves up to receiving His life-giving truth.

I saw myself hitting this huge **RESET** button and starting over from scratch. I gave permission to God, Jesus and Holy Spirit to begin teaching me the truth from their perspectives and requested all new lenses and filters. I erased all my old ways of thinking and understanding of who I believed God, Jesus and Holy Spirit were based on the perspective of my parents and my religious upbringing and chose to open the door to experience who they truly were, are and will always be... LOVE, PEACE AND GRACE.

I asked if I could have new eyes to see, new ears to hear and a whole new heart to receive. I made the conscious effort daily, to surrender and humble myself so I could be in a posture to receive. As time went by and I daily practiced the art of humility and surrender, I became very aware of when I was stepping into an old religious mindset or my new relational one. As I yearned for Him, I learned from Him. As I yielded my heart, spirit and soul over to each; Jesus, Holy Spirit and Father God, I began learning the art of true surrender.

Yielding and yearning are two beautiful words of surrender. As I yielded to Him, I yearned for more of Him and as I yearned, I learned.

Here are a few truths about God I discovered once I changed my own perspective; the foggy lens I was looking through and entered an intimate relationship with Him.

- His arms are always opened to receive you.
- There is nothing He can't handle.
- Regardless of what you have done or what you are going to do, He just loves you.
- He does not look at you and see your sin, He sees a child whom He loves.
- He can be trusted, and He has your best in mind.
- You cannot surprise Him, He already knows.
- He is always available 24/7 and longs to have a personal and intimate relationship with you.
- He does not own a day planner, calendar or measuring stick.
- He is never late, will not show up or cancel on you.

- He is a God of breakthrough and circumstantial turnaround.
- He wants us to receive breakthrough and healing more than we want it for ourselves.
- He practices healthy boundaries.
- He is not an enabler but desires for you to learn, grow and be empowered.
- He will never leave you behind, forget about or abandon you.
- He is never too busy for you.
- He is never disappointed in you.
- He believes in you, always has and always will.

When I finally accepted and received these truths about my heavenly Dad and discovered the reality of how He viewed me; not only was our relationship drastically changed but I was too. My worth and value began to change, and I no longer looked to the world for my value, worth or purpose. I now had a Dad that longed and passionately sought after me because He loved me, is for me, and I no longer needed to morph into someone else because I finally accepted me based on Gods acceptance of me. This new perspective was transformational for me and continues to transform me to this very day. It allowed me to experience intimacy in a whole new way and on a whole new level. This revelation was the key to recognizing the welcoming mat to His door of transformational healing.

As I engaged and opened myself up to encounter God, Jesus and Holy Spirit in an intimate way, they began presenting opportunities for deeper enlightenment and healing. My part was to submit, knowing the door was always open to enter in and receive what was waiting and available to me on the other side. *Matthew 7:7-8 says it all; "Ask and it will be given to you; seek and you will find; knock and the door will be opened to you."* In this verse it does not say maybe or possibly, it says… **WILL.** God is a God that does not go back on His word or change His mind, so what is written even if it was 2000 years ago still stands as truth today. His healing is always available to all of us, we just need to choose to enter in and receive it.

When I had my encounter with Jesus in my bedroom, I knew the road ahead of me was not going to be easy, but I also knew it would be well worth it in the long run and that I was not doing it alone. That day I made a promise to God to be obedient to and only worship Him and to fight for me, all of me. I knew that I had to wipe clean the old ways of thinking so to receive a new way. I longed to relearn everything but from His perspective because He is the best parent ever. It was the start of a friendship and almost 8 years later, it has blossomed into a beautiful courtship. Let me reassure you of one thing, once you begin seeking out God for a more meaningful relationship and His perfect perspective, He will show up because He is a God of relationship; A God of Love who desires to interact with you, to bond and be intimate with you. He is not a one-night stand.

Changing Perspective

Over the last 7+ years, there have been many times I have been triggered and quickly resorted back to my wounded self; which in the natural took on the form of reacting instead of responding in love. Instead of berating myself, criticizing who I am or giving up on myself, I took it as another challenge and door opening to watch as God perfectly loved on me by exposing the pain so to get rid of it once and for all. When these opportunities arose, I could almost feel Him hugging and kissing me. I recall this one time choosing to become overwhelmed by my circumstances and the emotions that came along with it. It did not take very long before I had gotten myself all worked up and was fuming inside. As I played the same record called "I can't believe he, she or they did that to me!" over and over in my head, I became more and more swallowed up by the toxic thoughts it produced and I soon felt like I was drowning and in many senses I was. I could sense the presence of Holy Spirit so leaned in and heard Him say… "You know what to do with this, I have taught you and you have taught on this yourself baby girl." He began showing me all my training about holding every thought captive and so almost by instinct; I threw up my hands in the natural as to reach for His in a gesture to say, "Help me, I am drowning here!" At that very second His hand grasped mine and I entered a vision and saw an eagle soaring through the sky. It was so beautiful and free. He began teaching me about this powerful bird and the significance and importance of our perspectives. Here is what He told me:

- This majestic bird has an aerial view and things that appear big to us are actually very small to Him. **Perspective**
- An eagle can see further due to the altitude he flies which gives him a different perspective, a different view. *Perspective*
- An eagle feels free soaring high and so even establishes his nest high above, so he is safe and further away from trouble. *Boundaries*

That quick yet powerful vision taught me so much. For starters, God is here with me; sees, hears and knows everything and that includes the best time to step in. I love how He waited until I asked for help. He is such a gentleman and like I have repeatedly said, not an enabler. I also learned a very valuable lesson and tool when it comes to toxic thinking and perspective; when my *stink'n think'n* gets me in a funk and back into my junk; it is best to stop, reevaluate and quickly get back up in my heavenly seat where I belong, so that I can get God's perspective. It is written that we are seated in heavenly places so in faith, I see myself doing just that. I find that the quicker this time lapse is of seat transfer, the better and the less damage is done.

Ephesians 2:6 - And God raised us up with Christ and seated us with him in the heavenly realms in Christ Jesus.

In other words, I am making the conscious effort and choice to get higher and go higher like the eagle and get a different perspective. I am instead choosing to control the thoughts in my brain not the other way around. I am choosing higher elevation and I choose every day to hold all my thoughts captive, not just a few, but all. I inspect them and then release the ones to Jesus that are toxic and not producing life within me. I do not allow the enemy a second to mess with my head because my brain is very important real estate that I value, love, protect and desire to take the best care of. I see it as a hand's off zone to the enemy. I choose to love myself enough to set very healthy boundaries and that includes with my own thoughts.

"There is nothing in a caterpillar that tells you it's going to be a butterfly."

R. Buckminster Fuller

A Butterfly's Perspective

I absolutely love butterflies, especially blue ones and God uses them to minister and teach me on a regular basis. It all began with an amazing dream I had one night over 15 years ago where a beautiful vibrant blue butterfly flitted around me and then landed onto my outstretched hand and stayed there. The dream was so real and the colors so beautiful that the moment I awoke, I looked up this type of blue butterfly I saw in my dream and discovered that it was a Blue Morpho and was rarely seen here in the states. I knew this blue goddess of the sky would play out in my life at some point and I also knew this dream was from God even though at the time, I was not following Him. It was not for almost another 8 years and after my encounter, that I began uncovering the significance of that dream and within a week had even changed the name of my salon from Hair by Marcia to Butterfly Blue. Today, it is my branding and I can't tell you how many times I have received gifts with blue butterflies on them and each one blesses me so.

Did you know that a caterpillar must completely die within its cocoon to then change into a butterfly? The caterpillar turns into a liquid substance first before transforming into a butterfly. They know deep within them that this is their calling and what is necessary for them to eventually fly. How many of us need to change our mindset about trusting God and the place He has us at? Do we view change as bad or scary and therefore avoid it? Are we too prideful to admit that we too need change so block the possibility of it ever happening? That would be like the butterfly disputing with God, believing He can become a butterfly on His own without entering His cocoon. How much of the circumstances we are facing is from choices we made in the first place? Change only occurs in our surroundings when we first change within ourselves.

I also discovered that the prophetic meaning for blue is: Heavenly, prophetic, Holy Spirit, grace, revelation, knowledge, the river of God and life-giving flow of The Holy Spirit. I love retaining knowledge that opens new revelation into the powerful handiwork of God.

I am going to step out on a limb here and ask a difficult but necessary question, one that I had to ask myself. My question for you to ponder is: How has it been working for me this far not changing? This is one of those moments when the reality of that question can sting a bit but also can bring about awareness that change is necessary. The awareness always came first before the healing came. The good news is that even though there is discomfort in change and initial stretching will hurt but will not harm you; comfort is right around the corner. Change comes when we get uncomfortable, vulnerable, real and transparent. It's not like we can trick God into believing something different about ourselves when He is God and knows all. No matter how much negotiating I did with God and myself, the truth was I needed to change not God.

I believe that when a caterpillar enters its cocoon the focus is not on the changes or struggle within the cocoon but on the final breakthrough. The caterpillar is doing what comes natural and does not question its Creator. I reflect on that perspective quite often as I have been going through my own transformation process. My focus stays on His face and trusts in His goodness so I can enter rest and stay at peace through my cocoon time. I do this because at times the struggle could consume me to the point of giving up before the healing occurs. I make the choice to once again change my perspective, my lens and my focus. Once I saw the beauty in the breakthrough is when I became more pliable and flexible so to receive and celebrate the process instead of rebel against it or throw up resistance walls.

The breakthrough is going to come if it becomes a goal and something you believe is attainable. I had to not only believe in myself but in the goodness and faithfulness of God to love me through it to the point of breakthrough and beyond. I had to constantly remind myself who I belonged to and who calls me His beloved daughter. God told me that if I belong to Him and He created everything so than I belong anywhere I choose to be. It's the same confidence that a butterfly has when it enters its cocoon. It is doing what God created it to do and it belongs there. This epiphany opened the door for me to accept myself where I am on my journey in life without any regrets or judgment. I am who I am and that is okay because my heavenly daddy says so. How about them apples? My stink'n think'n which produced feelings of "not fitting in", "not belonging" or "not good enough" still showed up from time to time, but I was able to quickly recognize them as toxic thoughts and soar like the eagle before they could unpack their bags and stay.

The more I pressed into intimacy with God, Jesus and Holy Spirit and *nurtured* those relationships, the easier it became to receive, accept and believe deep within my heart, spirit and soul the words my heavenly family were saying to me rather than the voices in my head trying to remind me of my past. They no longer were just words, they were now truths and this truth is what began repairing many of the wounds in my spirit, soul and heart from those 30 years of wilderness wandering. As I received and accepted this new mindset, perspective and identity, change was inevitable, and my time in my cocoon became a time of celebration, renewal, restoration and ultimate redemption. I welcomed and accepted this beautiful process because in the end I knew it would develop within me character that would bring about positive life altering outcomes.

Romans 5:3-5 says it best. "We can rejoice, too, when we run into problems and trials, for we know that they help us develop endurance. And endurance develops strength of character, and character strengthens our confident hope of salvation. And this hope will not lead to disappointment. For we know how dearly God loves us, because he has given us the Holy Spirit to fill our hearts with his love."

I can only speak for myself here, but I was so ready for change and was done with not only my *stink'n think'n* but my wounded self, calling all the shots and wrecking my life. I was ready and willing for the challenges; the uncomfortableness through the process and the at times, painful stretching that was oh so necessary for the inner growth and healing to occur. It is because of this uncomfortable yet necessary time in my cocoon that I was able to transform in so many areas of my life and am continuing to transform even today. *The cocoon time is necessary for the change to come.* I had to die first of myself like the caterpillar for new life to be birthed deep within me.

For me, I have grown to love my cocoon time and look forward to the additional teaching and transformation I will receive. Through this process I have learned so many new things about my authentic identity; my authentic self, that I today own and celebrate. I began seeing myself valuable, worthy and precious, not broken, rejected, alone or shameful. The confidence I have received from this cocoon time has developed within me a deeper passion for intimacy and engagement with my heavenly family and a longing to love on myself even more. I know as I love on me, I love on God because He lives within me. As I love on me and take care of me during this beautiful process, I am worshiping my creator who created me. I am saying to Him, that He did a good job and I love Him for creating me. It is during this cocoon time that I have grown in knowledge and wisdom and humility to even be able to say that.

"We cannot move forward in our God-given destiny when we believe lies about ourselves and God."

M.A. Congdon

The old Marcia Ann was blinded to those truths because if she was aware of them, she might not have made the choices she had.

There was no way I loved myself by having zero boundaries and being with all those men. As I continue to transform in my cocoon of love and awareness, the most beautiful and precious gift to me from God is that I now see myself as He sees me which means I finally see myself separate from my past. This separation has allowed me to step in the direction of my purpose and calling and away from what once held me back. This adjustment to my mindset and perspective impacted everything within me and around me and lines up with the meaning of the cross. It is finished! He died for all my transgressions not a few here and there. To hang on to my past wounds, shortcomings and failures are basically saying that His time on the cross was pointless and not good enough for me.

Challenge:

In what areas in your life do you need breakthrough? (Defined as: A *sudden, dramatic, and important discovery or development*).

Relational   Spiritual

Financial   Emotional

Physical   All the above

- What does your breakthrough look like? Can you see it? Can you see yourself healed? If you can see it, now try to feel it within your heart and become excited about it. (Seeing it is your first step towards redemption, Awareness leads to wholeness.)
- Can you imagine yourself flying free on the other side? How does that feel? What would it be like to be free of doubt and fear? Shame and regret? Rejection or Oppression?
- Are you willing to yield to the promptings of The Holy Spirit and get uncomfortable for Jesus?
- Are you willing to take steps in achieving your breakthrough? If so, what would these steps look like?
- Are you willing to stick to a plan and see it through to completion?

Write down your steps and make sure they are reachable and reasonable. Your first step might be just being aware that you need to change your thinking. If you make each step too complicated, you might wind up giving up before reaching your goals or breakthrough. I want to encourage you to not give up and keep pressing into your breakthrough whether it is spiritual, financial, relational, physical or all four. A very important key here is to see your breakthrough happening and then allow it to move to your heart. Engage both your brain and your heart, knowing and feeling the magnificent presence of Christ alive within you, releasing to you the strength to reach and achieve it. I had to come into agreement and alignment with what God was saying about me for everything else to follow suit. Once my brain came into agreement with God, I then released it to enter my heart so I could feel the excitement of what was going to take place as I committed to inner healing and going after each breakthrough. I began imagining myself free and then began thanking God for what I desired before it even happened.

- If I believed I was a failure, an outcast, unlovable or not capable, I would be just that.
- If I believed men and love cause me pain and cannot be trusted, I would continue to produce that in my relationships with men.
- If I believed I was not capable of success or seeing an assignment to completion, then I would do neither and possibly reject opportunities due to those beliefs.

My first breakthrough came when I became vulnerable and obedient in my bedroom and since then, I have lost count of how many breakthrough moments I have experienced. I have faith in my heavenly dad who is The Father of breakthroughs, perfect love, redemption, resurrection, creation and change.

A great tool to use for growth awareness and steps to change with your own personal growth is *S.M.A.R.T.* goals. Be *Specific* - (well defined and clear). Make it *Measurable* - (How will you know the goal is completed or not). Make it *Attainable* – (Don't set a goal that you are unable to reach and will only frustrate you). Is it *Relevant*? (The goal benefits you not someone else). And last but not at all least, *Time-Based* – (When will the goal need to be completed by?)

I want to encourage you to begin a journal to keep record of your new mindset changes, goals and breakthroughs whether short term or long term that you desire to see happen in your life. Begin and form new habits of praying, asking for Gods perspective, writing everything down and then taking the steps to see it through. Writing everything down does make a difference and almost sets things into motion, the activation part. Visualize, write and speak your breakthrough out.

Professional athletes see their games, their plays, their challenges being played out in their head like a movie first before the actual day of competition. Focus in on your goal, your breakthrough happening and Jesus standing there at the finish line rooting you on. Allow yourself to feel the excitement knowing you achieved what you set out to achieve. Try not to resist this part if you are uncomfortable with feeling. I had to work through this since feelings were bad to me too. I had to give myself permission to feel and it became easier the more I practiced. I reminded myself that it was safe and nothing bad was going to happen if I allowed myself to feel. My goal has been to change so change would be birthed around me. I kept my eye on the goal and the prize which was breakthrough and freedom. Make no doubt; there will be an awakening inside you that will see it through to the end. *Change happens when we choose to change.*

Challenge:

Take a moment to reflect on a pattern you have with your thinking, a cycle or a path you continue to go on and down. Example: Do you tend to self-sabotage? If so, breakthrough is needed because the root will be a lie you believe. Self-sabotaging is a cycle which will need to be broken for your outcomes to change. Do you continue to attract to you controlling men/women? There is a judgment there against one or both parents that result in this cycle continuing to play out in your adult relationships. Ask Holy Spirit the following: (The goal here is to get a different perspective). Write it down.

- What lie, or toxic thought am I believing?
- When did I partner with this lie? (Typically, a memory will come to mind.)
- Who do I need to forgive? (Choose forgiveness because it is for you). Forgive whoever He shows you and this might be yourself.)
- Did I cast judgements on this person(s) resulting in reaping of said judgments?
- Whatever age you are when this one memory happened, engage with that child within and allow the child to forgive, not your adult self. (This might take time based on the level of pain within this memory. If your inner child is not ready to forgive, you need to allow them grace during this process. Take time to just validate and comfort until they trust you enough to let go and release the person(s) you as a child are choosing to hold in contempt. It is important to plant seeds of grace here so you can reap grace too. No one is perfect; sin is sin to God and He has

no sin scale. We forgive because we too have sinned, fallen short and need forgiveness.

I want to encourage you to walk through these steps for each toxic memory Holy Spirit shows you. Each memory He highlights to you is an area breakthrough is needed. Each breakthrough will birth change in your present and future circumstances. The next step in this breakthrough process is to hear the truth based on a heavenly perspective and then speak it out over yourself. You are replacing the lie with His truth.

Now Ask Jesus:

What are the truths? Write all the truths down and begin speaking them out any time the lie pops back up in your head. (Flush, release and receive; remember the toilet?)

The truth is what we need to grab ahold of and become partners with. The truth is what we need to replace the lie within our spirit and soul - (our mind, will and emotions). It is so important to replace the lie with the truth because it is within this exchange that new growth happens which leads to fullness and complete restoration. As we choose to do this, we are basically allowing Jesus to speak life back into our hearts, spirits and souls. This is a process the bible refers to as the renewing of our minds and a transformation of our spirit and souls.

Take time to praise God for exposing the lie and if willing, repeat the prayer below for believing the lie in the first place. It is always important to repent because it demonstrates humility which is a powerful gift established at the cross. *Forgiveness brings the power of the cross into our circumstance* which is why the enemy hates it. Here is a short prayer of repentance you can use if you like.

I want to first reiterate that there is no shame, guilt or condemnation here so if you are feeling any, dust yourself off. Grab ahold of His truth that He is here with you through all of this, He is crazy about you and He knows the truth, sees the breakthrough and you already at the finish line, and is here to guide you to it.

I repent Lord for believing the lie; _____.
I renounce this lie and place this lie into the loving arms of my savior, Jesus Christ. (Picture yourself doing this). I ask for your forgiveness and I release this lie completely to you. As you wash me clean from the side effects of this lie, purify my heart, my mind, my soul and my spirit with the blood of Jesus. Wash my thoughts clean and renew my mind with the truth of what you say about me which is _____. I demand that whatever the enemy has stolen from me due to this lie must be returned sevenfold in Jesus name. Amen! (You can be specific here about exactly what you demand returned). For example, if joy was stolen, ask for joy back.

John 19: 28-30 - Jesus knew that his mission was now finished, and to fulfill Scripture he said, "I am thirsty." A jar of sour wine was sitting there, so they soaked a sponge in it, put it on a hyssop branch, and held it up to his lips. When Jesus had tasted it, he said, "It is finished!" Then he bowed his head and gave up his spirit.

I have included a chart for you to fill out, if you choose, so you can see for yourself the lies you possibly believe verses the truth God wants you to know to replace the lie with. Typically, the cycles and patterns we have are a result of certain lies we believe. You might be able to see why you did what you did or believe what you believed based on the lies you have believed whether about God, yourself or others.

	LIE/FALSE BELIEF	**TRUTH**
GOD		
JESUS		
HOLY SPIRIT		

MYSELF		
MY PARENTS		
OTHERS		

Step III. Transformation through Forgiveness

The Freeing Power of Forgiveness

There is such great power in forgiveness because it represents what Jesus accomplished on the cross. When we forgive, we release that same power into our own lives and into the life of the one we chose to forgive. It is transformational to say the least.

We produce in our relationships what we believe in our hearts to be true.

Marcia Ann Congdon

Forgiveness is beautiful and opens the door to freedom and transformation within us and like the ripple effect I spoke about earlier, impacts other areas of our lives. It restores, renews and repairs not only our life but the lives of others around us as we experience the mighty transformational hand of Jehovah Shalom massaging away deadly debris within our heart. The condition of our heart will affect those closest in our lives and *we will produce in all our relationships what we believe in our heart to be true.* However, if we choose to not forgive, we choose to stay imprisoned to the pain we are carrying within us and this pain will be released in our responses, attitudes and actions towards others. We are also choosing to hold the ones we struggle to forgive captive and under contempt of our own court and who or what gives us the power to do that?

Galatians 3:13-14NIV - Christ redeemed us from the curse of the law by becoming a curse for us, for it is written: "Cursed is everyone who is hung on a pole." He redeemed us in order that the blessing given to Abraham might come to the Gentiles through Christ Jesus, so that by faith we might receive the promise of the Spirit.

I have never been in jail, but I do know that when you are a true prisoner, you are not capable of leaving prison unless a judge decides you are innocent and sets you free. In the case of unforgiveness, we are choosing to stay locked up in our prison cell of bitterness, resentment, anger and even hate. This unresolved pain can even lead to a position of pride where we refuse to forgive as payback to the person who we believe harmed or wronged us, as if they owe us.

No one owes us anything when Jesus paid for it all on the cross. I needed to get over myself and recognize that sin is sin to God and my sin just looks different from theirs. Therefore, who am I to hold any grudges or judgements when I myself have wounded plenty of people in my life and possibly due to the pain I chose to hang onto. As I took on a different perspective by leaning upon Jesus as my way of engaging with ultimate truth and redemption, what I discovered is that we are all imperfect and have wounded areas within us that can wound others. It is within us since the beginning of time and we need to understand that God loves us all regardless of the sins we produced while alive here on earth. He is a God of connection, so He desires to connect, and He does not allow our imperfections to stand in the way, we do.

What I discovered on this healing journey is that as I chose to stay *offended by,* and hold grudges against people I believed *hurt me;* I was allowing this person(s) who I believed owed me from my childhood or adult life, additional power into my life today. Therefore, I am choosing to give my power over to said person(s) whether they are still in my life or not. I am still allowing them to control me due the unforgiveness in *my* heart.

That's the thing about unforgiveness; we think we are punishing the other person when in fact we are punishing ourselves. Our heart, body and mind are being contaminated, not theirs. I understand that there are different levels of emotional pain just like there are different levels of physical pain, and if you were not heard or justified can bring about a need for justice or a need for revenge based on the level of emotional or physical pain. Will someone even hear my side? Will someone even try and understand me? Why are they getting away with what they did to me? I understand all sides of that and what I discovered along the way is; *so does Jesus*. He understands too.

As I processed through the wounded areas of my heart where loss, rejection, fear, anger and shame once lived; He would always respond to me by saying; He understood, and you know what? He does! I cannot imagine what He felt while He was alive on this planet. All the people who came against Him and verbalized that disagreement at Him. He was shamed, betrayed by one of His friends, tormented, ridiculed, spit upon, clothes ripped, humiliated, whipped, hung on a cross even though innocent, and rejected by His dear friends as He endured the pain while on the cross. Even today, He is still rejected. He does get it and that alone gave me validation and peace, and eased the areas within me that still needed to be heard and understood.

The bottom line here is that forgiveness is for you and you are only doing yourself an injustice by hanging onto the memory of the pain. The longer the pain sits there, the longer you allow it to eat away at your heart, mind, spirit, soul and Yes, your body. Anger, resentment and bitterness are all negative emotions and produce negative energy within your body. By not forgiving, you are then choosing to hang onto all that negative energy, you are allowing it to affect your physical body and it will. Please hear me when I say that burying it deep inside does not mean you have dealt with it; it means you have buried it deep inside so not to deal with it.

I cannot express enough the importance of recognizing the needs of your inner child, allowing her/him to heal through recognition of said wounds and receive your healing through forgiveness. Until this happens, you will continue to go through life allowing those wounds to lead and contaminate your adult self and anyone you are throwing up on due to those wounds not healed. The only way to enter the doorway of freedom is to recognize and deal with the pain, forgive and let go. It's not a magic trick, now you see it, now you don't. We need to allow ourselves time to grieve the loss the child inside us experienced, mourn if we need to mourn, yell if we need to yell and then forgive the person(s) involved and release it all to Jesus. There is no spoon full of sugar to help this go down, gosh I love Mary Poppins and wish it was that easy. However, it does require commitment, grit and grace to see it through to the end, but the rewards you will receive will catapult you into a life where you do understand, witness and experience life from His fullness of grace, peace, mercy, joy and love.

Psalm 16:11TPT - For you bring me a continual revelation of resurrection life, the path to the bliss that brings me face-to-face with you.

During a very painful time in my teenage years, exactly 6 months before I became pregnant, I chose to make some serious vows and verbal covenants with anger, hate, bitterness and resentment. What I believed in my heart to be true and spoke out did come to pass and I spoke many things out that were downright mean and mainly about what I thought of love, life, my parents, being good and about me. I spoke out loud and in anger many "I will never's!" "I'll show them what bad looks like! "and "I am such a _____!" statements and came into agreement with each one of them.

That night in my bedroom became the birthplace of something ugly inside of me that contaminated my life until Holy Spirit made me *aware* and freed me of her. I cannot express the importance of the words and covenants you make when angry. I was so angry that I agreed to never being good again and was pregnant 6 months later. The angry thoughts did not just stay within my mind, I allowed them to corrupt and pierce my heart and I produced in my life the ugliness that lived within me. Once again, this was my 18-year old perspective of the dilemma I allowed to corrupt me. Just because I saw it this way did not mean everyone else involved did. If there are 3 people involved in a dilemma, there are 3 different perspectives. I think you get my point here.

I want to challenge and encourage you to forgive, but I also want to encourage you to forgive from the age you were wounded. In the above trauma which occurred just 1 month after my sudden breakup with prince, I was already an emotional wreck so this trauma so soon after the last sent me over the edge and the anger I had that night corrupted me until I went back and freed myself from my 18-year old's need to punish everyone who she believed was controlling her or trying to cause her harm.

Looking back at the pain my heart was experiencing that night in my bedroom, I believe my young 18-year old had a nervous breakdown. From her young and wounded perspective, her world was falling apart, and she had no idea how to cope with any of it, so she didn't.

A wounded perspective is the reality of the wounded person.

She was out for justice and if she believed someone was trying to wrong her, you better watch out. She became my protector and I had no idea I had allowed such a thing to happen until I went back and spoke with her alongside Jesus. When Holy Spirit brought this memory back up to me a 3rd time, I questioned Him since I had thought that I had already dealt with this memory but apparently there was more, and He knew just what. I had already in the past taken the time to forgive my parents for allowing my twin to go to our High School graduation party, but not me. I had forgiven them so many times, I had lost count. Apparently, my 18-year old self had not and was still quite ticked off.

It all began while traveling on this new pathway of inner healing. I was diligently working on my areas of PTSD and the triggers I recognized that produced rage inside me. I had noticed that I continued to get triggered when I felt wrongly accused and my outburst would go from zero to 10 in seconds flat and I had zero filters and boundaries with what was spewing from my mouth. As I became aware of this trigger and the anger raging inside me, I asked Holy Spirit to show me the wound because I knew something was up.

He immediately showed me a memory of the night I was planning on going to my high school graduation party to say goodbye to all my friends and at the last minute was told I could not. I looked a bit puzzled since I believed I had already walked through all the forgiveness prayers but trusted Holy Spirit so agreed to go back and take another look and see what I might have missed the first 2 times. I chose to love myself enough to go back to the memory; engage with my 18-year old self, hear and validate her as she explained why she was so angry, try and help her process through her anger and fear by hearing, nurturing, comforting and encouraging her to let all the pain go for her sake.

As I followed the promptings of The Holy spirit, I discovered that my 18-year old self believed she still needed to protect me because apparently, I was too nice and allowed people to bully me and walk all over me. Even though I tried to coax her to step aside, she was not so willing to believe that I did not need her anymore. She was still quite upset by the way she had been treated and believed not only that people were out to get her, but that being nice meant you were weak and would be taken advantage of.

As I continued to listen to her, validate her and encourage her to hand this pain over to Jesus, some of the resistance walls began coming down and she shared that she believed that she MISSED OUT ON LIFE. When her sweet heart poured those words out of them, I felt the lightbulbs going off within me and chains breaking. That was a chain-breaking truth and it felt so good to release that lie from within my heart so my circumstances could begin changing today.

There was still a great deal of anger and a need to protect so I continued to trust Holy Spirit here and He prompted me to assume my position today as a God-fearing, anointed Daughter of The King and inform my 18-year old that I love her, but I do not need her services any longer and that God was my protector and takes very good care of me. I then introduced her to Jesus and told her that she could trust Him and sent her on her way with Him. Wow! That was one crazy intervention but one very necessary for me as a 56-year-old woman to be free and not continue to be contaminated and in many senses controlled by my 18-year old ticked-off self who still wanted vengeance for the wrong she believed had been done to her.

Jesus then showed me that at 18, I had positioned myself as god by my need for justice and my need for vengeance. (Ouch moment!) I had to release all judgement and need for justice over to His open arms because it was not mine to take. I also realized how much fear there was behind this anger and gave that to Him as well in exchange for His divine peace that surpasses all understanding, is perfect and casts out all fear.

Romans 12:19 - "Do not take revenge, my dear friends, but leave room for God's wrath, for it is written: 'It is mine to avenge; I will repay,' says the Lord."

As this intervention came to an end, Jesus released revelation to me by showing me exactly how this judgment and toxic mindset played out in my life and my adult-self began to weep. As I allowed myself to release this pain stored up within me for years, my weeping increased, and a guttural cry came out and at that moment I felt completely free. I had held onto this false belief, this toxic lie and poisonous mindset for way too long and that day, Jesus loved me to a new level of wholeness.

You see, instead of celebrating the life I was living, I took on a perspective of victim and this is the filter I viewed life from. Since I had chosen to make partners with my pain that night, cast all sorts of judgements against my parents and believed and accepted as truth that being nice gets you nowhere, love is painful, people were out to get me and that I was missing out on life; that is exactly what I produced until that very day, when Jesus set me free.

I produced it in my marriages, my friendships and with family members. My young 18-year old self believed she had missed out on true love with Prince, celebrating her graduation, saying farewell to her high school friends, her young adult-life-since she was pregnant and a mom, and experiencing a fun and care-free life as a young adult. And the sad truth is that due to my judgments and poisonous perspectives, I missed out on so many beautiful moments every single day because my focus stayed on the pain in my past and that pain dictated the outcomes of my life. Did I miss out? You bet I did! That is exactly what I believed would happen so that is exactly what I produced, so I could prove myself right. I missed out on joy, laughter, happiness, contentment, peace, love, kindness; to name a few because I was too consumed with the pain to see the blessings spilling out in front of me.

Please be open and try to understand judgments and unforgiveness and how they can continue to contaminate your life unless you break free of them through forgiveness and repentance. I cannot get any of those years back and if I was still living with a victim mindset, could possibly become overtaken by that too, but instead I see it as victory and look forward to the days and years ahead as a free woman, a butterfly with her wings, an eagle soaring high above the clouds taking in all of God's creation and celebrating and welcoming each day as a gift.

Each phase of this inner transformational healing journey required me being good to me. I am repeating myself here and that is okay, but forgiveness is for you. I had to finally die of myself, swallow my pride and choose to forgive all person(s) throughout my life for what I believed was their part in inflicting their own brokenness and pain onto me. Even if they released their pain onto me, does not mean I needed to receive and own it myself. I assume full responsibility for allowing myself to take it on, own it and carry it around. I chose to own their stuff when it wasn't mine to own. I gave them that power; they did not take it from me. I chose to take it personal, to take offense and give them so much importance that it altered the way I looked at myself, made decisions in life and how I treated others. I have learned on this journey of wholeness and sanctification that they too are possibly wounded and living from their own wounded perspectives, just like I did. Their own perspective might have been clouded by painful memories just like mine, so once again, who am I to judge them? What gives me that right?

It is so important to recognize who you are up against here and who is trying to confuse you. Who is trying to steal from you? Your flesh is going to want to hold onto the hurt and this is where the enemy will work. I grew the most when I realized that I needed to see the sin separate from the sinner. Sin is sin and it is flesh driven. Jesus was the only person who walked this earth without sin even though He was tempted in every area. People will sin and let you down just like I have sinned and let people down. When we show grace and forgive, we are partnering with God's loving heart and we are planting great seeds that will impact our lives. It is such an amazing feeling when you can release a person, yourself included and the pain you believe they caused you into the arms of Jesus with confidence knowing He has it and you no longer need to carry it.

If that is not enough to help you choose to forgive; like I mentioned earlier, unforgiveness will damage your body too. It causes negative emotions, (energy) within you that can lead to sleepless nights, digestive issues, ulcers, confusion, high blood pressure, strokes, joint disorders, fibromyalgia, immune disorders, anxiety, depression, etc. And if you cope with all your pain by eating, drinking, viewing porn, sex, not eating, shopping, gambling, etc.; that too will damage your body and life. Your body will be affected by the pain of your unforgiveness. Let it go and let God deal with it. I realize that sounds so cliché, but it is the truth. His hands are very large and there is nothing that surprises Him or that He can't handle.

Our bodies were not created to carry pain. God refers to our bodies as temples of His and we are to take care of these temples. Taking care of our temples does not mean that we own everybody's pain, feelings and hang onto it all until we are sick ourselves. How can we even begin to glorify or honor God with our bodies if we are carrying so much resentment and pain? *Jesus already took all our sin and our pain to the cross, so it is not ours to carry if He already did.* Please reread that over and over until it sinks in and you internalize it.

1 Corinthians 6:19-20 - Don't you realize that your body is the temple of the Holy Spirit, who lives in you and was given to you by God? You do not belong to yourself, for God bought you with a high price. So, you must honor God with your body.

Ezekiel 36:26 - I will give you a new heart and put a new spirit in you; I will remove from your heart of stone and give you a heart of flesh.

Matthew 11:28-30 - "Come to me, all you who are weary and burdened, and I will give you rest. Take my yoke upon you and learn from me, for I am gentle and humble in heart, and you will find rest for your souls. For my yoke is easy and my burden is light."

Forgiveness and our Connection with God

As I relentlessly and passionately pursued restoration and inner transformation, I have discovered that there is a link between forgiveness and unlocking connection with our heavenly family. I love using analogies and this one might not be understood by those born with all our new

technology. When I was growing up, we had dial-up phones and there was the one phone for the entire household. You would need to wait your turn to use the phone and as a teenager; sharing the house with 3 other teens, at times this became very frustrating. In addition, there were many times the connection was bad due to storms and you had to try and hear the other person with all this static on the line. This is how I see unforgiveness regarding our connection to God, Jesus and Holy Spirit. All our unforgiveness can cause static and in many cases complete disconnection with them. I have found that the more I forgave; the more clutter was removed and there would be an increase in His presence and the clarity of His voice. I love how I never need to wait to talk to Him either. He's always available and so desires to chat.

I do not believe there is any other way to achieve complete inner peace and sanctification without it. If you are ready and willing, the challenges below will not only release peace into your life through forgiveness, but I believe will open the doors of communication between you and your heavenly family. Remember, forgiveness is for you not the other person(s). Yes, I said it again.

Challenge:

Walking out forgiveness; the use of forgiveness tools. Time to be challenged, IF……

- You feel ready to forgive someone you believe has hurt or offended you.
- You are ready to move forward and not be held back by unforgiveness.
- You are ready to enter a deeper, more intimate connection with God, Jesus and Holy Spirit.
- You are ready to take your power back.

First things first… Praise God and way to go! Begin first with a minute of praise, thanksgiving and worship. This sets the stage for what is to come and helps prepare your heart. It's like warming up your muscles before exercising. Grab some paper and a pen and document everything.

Heavenly Father, thank you, for your gift of forgiveness and how beautifully Jesus demonstrated it on the cross. Thank you for the power that was released on the cross that day to set all your children free. I choose today to partner with that amazing gift as I walk through my own forgiveness. Jesus, I ask for you to be here with me and give me the strength I need to walk this out. Holy Spirit will you comfort me where I need comforting. In Jesus name I pray. Amen.

Transformation Tool #1

Begin by asking Jesus, *who am I struggling to forgive? Why?* Once you have that person in mind, ask Him the following and I suggest writing it down. (Repeat sequence of questions with each person Jesus shows you and you choose to forgive, and this includes you if you still need to forgive yourself).

1. Jesus, how do you see this person? (I had to get His perspective at times in order to forgive).
2. Jesus, tell me something about their heart that I do not know and might not choose to see due to my unforgiveness hindering my perspective?
3. Jesus, what lie have I believed about this person? (Due to my pain)
4. Jesus, what is the truth about this person? (His perspective will always be kind).

If by chance you receive a bad image or word, flip it to be positive. Gods view is always from a place of pure and perfect love. Just as we can hear and then believe lies about ourselves, we can also hear and believe lies about others. God puts things in pure perspective and will only speak His truth. When we hear or see negative, it can be our twist or whatever unclean thought we are entertaining causing interference.

Once you receive Gods perspective about the person you are struggling to forgive, are you ready to release them over to His arms and out of yours? If so, below is a very simple prayer you can pray for each person He has shown you still need to forgive and release. Remember this is a process you are going through, so be good to you here; listen to your body, your heart, mind and spirit and when enough is enough, stop and rest. I also want to encourage you to forgive from the age the pain was introduced, so give the adult in you permission to release any need to control. Remember, there is no time limit, no stop watches, and no grades. God is a patient and loving God and will not push you or try to control you; He will always give you a free will and allow you to go at your own pace.

A few reminders:

- Be good to yourself here, nurture yourself.
- Take the time you need to walk this through.
- Show yourself grace, it does not need to be rushed.
- You are not being graded.
- Progress not perfection

Father, today I choose to forgive _____ for _____.
(Be specific here with why you need to forgive). I choose today to release all judgement I have made against _____. Please forgive me for hanging onto this unforgiveness for so long and for any judgement I wrongly made against them due to my pain. Please release the pain from within my body that I chose to hang onto and restore my body by breathing life back into it. I ask this in the mighty and powerful name of Jesus, Amen.

After you have walked through some forgiveness prayers please take time to celebrate and pat yourself on the back. Hear God saying, "Well done my good and faithful son/daughter!" Know that your heavenly family is celebrating alongside you and are very proud of you. Celebrate with them and be proud of yourself, this is a victory! Give yourself a gold star! You've done well!!

Matthew 25:21 - "His master replied, well done, good and faithful servant! You have been faithful with a few things; I will put you in charge of many things. Come and share your master's happiness!'

Transformation Tool #2

A very successful transformation tool God has me use after I have gone through the 1st one is to then begin speaking blessings over them. Boy, this one challenged me when the pain was still raw. This is part of the sifting, stretching and shifting that can be uncomfortable but necessary. I had to remind myself continually of the goal, which was to be set free so to move forward and establish change in my life circumstances. Choosing to not forgive will keep you in the past and away from experiencing complete joy in your present and future moments to come.

One of the hardest things to do when we have been deeply wounded is to thank God for the person(s) who hurt us and ask Him to bless them. Why would I want to do that when I believe they are the ones responsible for my pain? The twist there is that we are the ones responsible for our own happiness, not them. We are also responsible for the way we see things and the lens we look through. If I continued to view them as terrible people who harmed me, I would not necessarily be able to forgive them and move on. I am also bowing down to the pain and the person(s) I believe subjected said pain upon me and allowing both to control my future. *If I place so much emphasis and importance on the pain, I believe they caused me then in a sense I am worshipping my pain and the person I received the pain from. The pain is still calling the shots, still determining my outcomes as is the person I believe inflicted the pain upon me.*

My prideful ways would convince me that they deserved to be punished and I was better off without them in my life. It is amazing the lies pride will whisper in your ear so you can remain in your junk and be okay with it. The truth of the matter is that we all sin and fall short so who are we then to hold anyone in contempt when we too have sinned? I had to face that truth in order to be able to begin forgiving and blessing without feeling like I was doing myself a disservice. *When we choose forgiveness, we are taking back our power.*

The first time I had heard about this tool was over lunch with a dear Christian girlfriend of mine about 6 months after my encounter and the sacrifice of the toxic relationship I chose to be in for 2-1/2 years. Even though I knew deep down I was being obedient to God by sacrificing that relationship, the pain at times still made an appearance, sometimes worse than others, and I continued to go back and forth with forgiveness and struggled totally letting it all go. I had grown to love him very much and had believed we would one day be married, so I was not only questioning myself but also trying to deal with the loss of the relationship, the loss of a dream I had for us, the betrayal knowing he had been already seeing someone else and the guilt and shame of choosing to go down that path in the first place. That's where shame comes back in if you allow it. Shame does not play fair and kept trying to remind me…. "You are bad because you made another bad relationship choice!" "You are such an idiot!" or even worse, "He is better off without you and that's why he chose someone else."

Thank goodness for this amazing friend of mine who took the time to love on me and was there to help encourage and build me up. God is a God that loves well and so in advance He had placed her back in my life about a month before the breakup and I am forever grateful to Him for that. Over our lunch, she prayed for me and God showed her this tool I just described. She also gave me *2 Corinthians 12:9* to memorize and declare from that day forward. *But He said to me, "My grace is sufficient for you, for my power is made perfect in weakness." Therefore, I will boast all the more gladly about my weaknesses, so that Christ's power may rest on me.* She handed me a pink sticky note with this scripture verse written on it and the date which was 9/23/12 and I still have it. She also spoke a blessing over me saying, and I quote; "By 9/23/13, a year from now; you will look back on your life and be amazed at what God has done." My husband and I were married on 9/21/13.

I trust the voice of God in this friend, so I knew what she was speaking was truth, and I knew deep down that her advice was necessary for me to heal. At first, it took every bit of strength I had to speak those words out. Jesus had to help me because I knew I couldn't do it without Him, that's the grace part in the above scripture verse. It was not easy praying blessings over this man when I wanted to drop kick him instead. I don't know about you but for me, grace and I kind of had this love/hate type of relationship. I loved and welcomed it when others showed me grace, but reciprocating was the challenge for me. *I realize how necessary it is to walk in grace because it is the existence of God being demonstrated through you when you do.* I also knew that as I planted seeds of grace, grace is what I will reap.

At this time in my life though, and with the level of emotional pain I was enduring, it did not come so easy and I continued to lean into His grace to get me through. There was no way I could show this man an ounce of grace without Gods assistance. Since I've always been an overcomer and someone who likes a good challenge, I kept focused on the finish line and the breakthrough; trusting my friend's sound advice and more importantly trusting God in me to do the rest. I knew that He would not lead me to this and then leave me. I knew and believed that He had much bigger plans for me than I did for myself, and this was the process I needed to be in for those plans to come to life. I also knew that there was no way I would be able to do something like this by myself, so I continued to show myself grace, be good to me and lean on Him. Once I chose to completely surrender it over to Him was when this process became so much easier to achieve. It was no longer by my strength but by Jesus within me. It's not by my stripes that I am healed but only by His!

Isaiah 53:5 - "But He was wounded for our transgressions, He was bruised for our iniquities; the chastisement for our peace was upon Him, and by His stripes we are healed."

It was a miracle God gave me because I looked past myself and my hurt and partnered with His love and grace. In time and without me being aware of it, the words I spoke out moved from my head to my heart. It did not happen overnight, by any means but it did happen. I soon became aware that as I continued to thank God and bless this person who I believed had hurt me, it became easier and easier. I even began asking God to bless his new relationship and that is when I knew a shift within me had taken place and I celebrated it. I realized I was saying it now from a place of forgiveness, sincerity, grace and mercy rather than rejection, duty, sadness or even hate. God is about restoration and making all things new. He was doing a new thing within my heart and I was not even aware of it. He saw the bigger picture way before I ever did and was taking the steps necessary to get me there.

The best part is that this practice of forgiveness brought me closer to my heavenly family and that is all that truly matters. It allowed additional walls to come down and decluttered the airways which helped me enter a deeper, more intimate relationship with God, Jesus and Holy Spirit. When we forgive, we are nurturing, honoring and loving our spirits and hearts back to health. Today, as I now write about this person, Praise God there is no pain, shame or anger. That is God's way of healing, restoring and His way of blessing my obedience. He heals the pain and because He is God, He can even remove all memory of the pain. That is what partnering with forgiveness can do for you. As you partner with forgiveness, you partner with God, His intentions, His plans and the power demonstrated on the cross.

If you are ready; below is a simple prayer of blessing over those you just allowed yourself to forgive.

Father, please bless _____'s life, their coming and their going. Bless their job, relationships, family and paths _____ chooses to take. Keep _____ safe from harm and protect _____ in the days to come. In Jesus name, Amen. (Breathe and receive another Gold star!) Good Job! Super proud of you!

Isaiah 43:18-19 - "Remember not the former things, nor consider the things of old. Behold, I am doing a new thing; now it springs forth, do you not perceive it? I will make a way in the wilderness and rivers in the desert."

Transformation Tool #3

While on the beautiful and freeing subject of forgiveness; self-forgiveness is a huge part of you becoming free from believing all the lies the enemy has been telling you about yourself. The enemy is the father of lies so that is what he does best, he lies! He desires to bring death and God desires to bring life. It's as simple as that.

If you have a hard time forgiving yourself, I understand. For so many years, way too many to even count; I stayed in a place of self-hatred, shame and contempt. I almost daily berated, insulted and had a negative outlook of myself. I had a hard time saying or hearing anything positive and that too is pride. To me, I deserved to be punished for my choices and took on not only a critical spirit but punishing spirit as well.

I had to relearn everything about love and healthy relationships since love, pain and punishment became one in the same. It took years of practicing new ways of loving, showing grace, connecting and stopping myself when I went to judge or be critical of myself or others. I had to relearn how to do everything the opposite of what I had been taught how to do. Instead of lashing out and punishing, I had to show grace and forgive. This was a very difficult and challenging area for me, and it became easier as I realized I was honoring God and demonstrating His character when I practiced humility instead of pride; forgave and did not punish by with-holding love.

To forgive myself was not something I even gave a second thought to. I knew and had heard plenty of times about the forgiveness of others but myself? I had no idea that I had taken on a martyr, defeated and victim mentality. I unknowingly was taking on a prideful stance believing that what Jesus did on the cross wasn't good enough for my sins. Like I had that much power to be excluded from what the word of God teaches? Pride, whether from an angle of weakness or strength, will keep us blinded to His truth. Pride is self-led while humility is selfless love, so less of self. We are to aim for being righteous in love, not self. One demonstrates humility and one pride.

Just as we need to forgive others and release the pain, we believe they caused, over to God; we also need to do the same for ourselves. Don't we deserve the same grace? Part of loving and nurturing ourselves is forgiving and releasing whatever our life's choices were over to God. As we love and honor ourselves with kindness, grace and compassion, we are doing the same to Jesus since He lives within us.

Here is a simple prayer of self-forgiveness you can choose to pray if you are willing to let yourself off the hook and off the cross.

Father God, I choose to forgive myself for _____. (list them all). I repent for all self-slander, self-hate, self-malice, and all negative thoughts I spoke against myself. I break any inner vows or word curses I spoke against myself in Jesus name. I release all judgement of myself into your loving arms. I ask that you deliver me of any critical or punishing spirit in Jesus name and refill my spirit with a spirit of humility and grace. I ask that you now cover me completely in the blood of Jesus and fill me up with your words of truth about how you see me.

Father God, what do you think about me? (Write this down and please receive each word of truth He says about you and begin speaking these truthful and life-giving words over and into yourself.) I choose to partner with you today Jesus to not only see myself as you do, but release to you my need to control by handing over to you the reigns, I have been carrying to do this thing called life. I choose this today in Jesus' name, Amen!

Every year, I have my rose bushes pruned so the next season they have an increase of blooms on them. The same goes with God pruning us. As He prunes away our old and dead blooms and branches during one season, the next season we will demonstrate a higher and deeper level of love, grace, peace, joy, hope and faith. Look at it and welcome it as the following pruning process:

- A new-found freedom from the lies of the enemy process.
- A refining of my heart process.
- A life redeemed process.
- A restoring of my heart and mind process.
- A sifting to shifting process.
- His glory to be revealed process.
- His sanctification process.

In Jesus name, I declare and decree over you, freedom doors opening, and your airways decluttered through your faithful act of forgiveness. I declare over you, new spiritual sight where you will begin recognizing the tangible presence of God, Jesus and Holy Spirit in your day to day life. I declare and decree miracles, signs and wonders to become something you are familiar and comfortable with. May the power of God resonate through you and may you accept the challenge of your calling He has placed upon your life to be fulfilled by you and with the assistance of heaven. Amen!

I also want to take a minute to bless your spirit as you begin this deeper relationship with your heavenly family and this new journey of discovery alongside them. Begin by placing your hand just below your chest and speak this blessing aloud over your spirit:

Spirit, I bless you to now be awakened in Jesus' name and come into agreement only with what Father God says about you. Spirit, it is time to rise and become fully awakened and aligned with the words spoken out by your heavenly family and receive all instruction and guidance from them alone. Spirit, be blessed to receive and accept the agape love from your heavenly Father, the brotherly love of Jesus and the comforting and wise counsel from The Holy Spirit. Spirit, step out of any agreement you have previously made from religious beliefs, fears, lies doubt, false perspectives and generational curses, and begin partnering with what your Father in heaven has written about you in your book of life and the words He speaks out about you every day in heaven. In Jesus' name, amen!

Over time, as Holy Spirit counseled me to reach new levels of inner healing and transformation, I began choosing to love myself for me and was okay with that. I then found myself desiring and believing that I deserved the kind of love only God could offer. I allowed myself to be reintroduced to and welcomed into my life His perfect love. I was able to forgive those that did not demonstrate that kind of love because I knew that I too, had fallen short in that area. It is such freedom when you can humble yourself enough to then see what the truth is. This requires dying of self and that is the gateway to inner healing and freedom. I began valuing myself so I could value others. You cannot give what you do not have. As I grew in love, honor, value, grace and respect for myself, I was then and only then able to demonstrate that to others.

Step IV: My Heavenly Dance of Intimacy

With Jesus

My dance of intimacy began with Jesus the moment the encounter happened. The encounter was the door being opened within my heart to discover Jesus as my husband not just The Son of God. I in turn, had to learn how to trust a man again and resist the urge to lead because my flesh wanted to be in control due to fear. He slowly began to teach me about His perspective of love and trust during our alone time together. He never pushed me too far or applied too much pressure. He was not controlling, dominating, obtrusive, disapproving, rude or negligent. The more time I spent with Him learning and growing in friendship and intimacy, the more I began discovering the true character of Jesus; how gentle, patient loving and kind He is.

Jesus began showing me what true courting looked like as He wooed me through the first steps of my open heart and spirit surgery. That season was what I call my "Teatime with Jesus" pruning season and was an important and necessary step I needed to learn in this dance of intimacy. I basically dated Jesus. I even went as far as purchasing a new welcome mat for my front porch step and blessed it as a sign that He is always welcomed in my home and in my heart. I would treat these encounters as dates, dress up and set the table for two, excited about what He had planned for the two of us.

As time went by, I grew and matured emotionally and spiritually and began getting more comfortable with these new dance steps I was learning with Jesus as my perfect dance partner. As my trust grew in Him, I relaxed, lowered many of my walls and began asking Him questions about Himself too. I was hungry for the truth and knew there was so much I needed to learn from Him; about Him. As I submitted more of my heart to Jesus and allowed Him to court me, I began experiencing for the first-time true intimacy that was safe and sex free.

He was always the perfect gentlemen and through this time of courtship, He taught me what self-respect, self-value, and self-worth looked like. He taught me how to be loved and to love from a place of humility, not a form of manipulation and control. He showed me that I am never alone which was huge for the orphan in me. He helped me to see myself as His bride; beautiful and spotless instead of broken and stained. This was our special time together I treasured and looked forward to. I didn't realize this then, but He was preparing my heart for my next marriage even though at the time, I was not interested in that.

Since He is a God that loves well, He very slowly and perfectly increased our time together and soon I too desired more. It wasn't until I grew in relationship with Jesus and allowed Him to be my husband, my best friend and at times my big brother, that I learned the truth about not only my own identity but the real meaning of love and courtship. I was able to break free of my fantasy world that was holding me back and came into agreement with His perspective and His heart for me and others. I broke up with shame and guilt and gave myself permission to grieve and even mourn all the losses I had experienced as a little girl, adolescent, young adult and adult so I could move forward into victory. I learned from Jesus the importance of surrender, sacrifice and service which He demonstrated so perfectly while living on this earth.

I had to relearn so many things regarding relationships, identity, sex, intimacy and marriage. The way I did things before I knew I could no longer do so I was up for any challenge He brought my way. This was a much-needed time in my healing journey, inside my cocoon and because of the sweet and precious time Jesus took with me; demonstrating what courtship, respect, honor and pure love looked like, I was able to recognize those same traits in my husband of today.

When I first met my husband Dave, I was at a Christian singles event I personally had planned with another Christian friend of mine. Since I was doing things differently now, I said good-bye to all dating sites, which enabled my sexual addiction and was just desiring healthy companionship with other Christians. Dave was attending this event only as the wingman for two of his bible-study friends. He himself was on a year sabbatical from dating, so to only focus on God.

Since I was the hostess, I politely shook his hand and introduced myself. Even though he was cute and had sweet eyes, I could not get past the huge handlebar mustache on his upper lip. The thing even was waxed and curled on the ends. Yikes! We wound up sitting next to each other at the restaurant and he was very quiet and I was busy trying to be a good hostess with the 30 people in attendance, so there was not a whole lot of chit chat between us and I was okay with that, I think we both were.

I managed to look past the Stache and accepted his request to be friends on Facebook, became his stylist, began sitting together at church and at times called each other up for prayer or just to talk and slowly, we became good friends. He was a super sweet guy, loved God with all his heart and on occasion would even stop by on his way home from work with some flowers or a homemade pie, he had just baked. I was not much of a pie eater but that does not mean I did not enjoy receiving them. He not only baked these pies for me, he would take the time to place butterflies on the crust knowing my love of them.

And then there was the time I mentioned to him that I had injured my lower back and my daughter too had a hurt shoulder. I had called him for prayers because I had bought tickets to see Cirque Du Soleil that night with both my daughters and was not sure if I could even drive due to the amount of pain, I was in. He called me later in the day to check on me and asked what time I would be heading out and if he could stop by because he had something for me. I figured it was another pie but none the less, told him the time of our planned departure. Well, to my surprise, he showed up on his way home from work and dropped off (3) three gift certificates for massages, one for me and one for each of my two daughters, he did not want to leave them out. My daughters and I all stood there like 3 deer's in headlights, in shock because they, like me had never seen such innocent sweetness before. He quickly excused himself since he knew we needed to go, and my daughters looked at me and said; "Mom! He's cute; you need to go out with him!" I answered them; "Oh No, not Dave, we are just friends, he is not my type."

Dave and I continued to be good friends and I continued believing he was not my type mainly due to him being almost 5 years younger, never having any children of his own and was too quiet and introverted. If by chance you have a list, throw it away! He had become wiser at least and decided to shave his Stache off which I was grateful for and told him so.

I decided to bake him lasagna since he was always baking me pies and I arranged to give it to him after church one Sunday night. We also planned on going to dinner afterwards to a local wing place with my youngest in tow.

I had arrived before him to church, found my seat and saved his next to me for when he would arrive. I was not quite prepared for what happened next; he calls it his Taser, but I call it God. I was sitting there, minding my own business and when he arrived and sat down our arms briefly touched and I felt this electricity run through me. I remember telling God; "It's Dave, we are just friends and remember, we have nothing in common!" Well, through the entire service, I had this ongoing conversation with myself and God, arguing why it could not possibly be Dave and then, God showed me why it could be, by reminding me about my special time with Jesus.

Service ended and we then met at the wing place with my daughter and had a great meal and conversation. Things were different for me because I still could not shake the sensation I experienced earlier at church and felt differently now while sitting across from him at the table. I started putting two and two together as a movie reel began playing out in my head of the similarities between the way Jesus courted me and Dave's sweet and kind heart over the last year. It began making sense and I for the first time considered myself worthy.

We were married 6 months later and because God is a God of redemption and makes all things new; stayed pure.

Even today as a married woman and Dave's beloved bride, I still allow Jesus to court me because He is still teaching me how to love Dave well. As I learn how to perfectly serve Jesus and receive love from Jesus, I am learning how to perfectly serve Dave and others. I am learning how to love by His example, which is perfect. Yes, I make mistakes and I resort to my old ways of trying to run at times, but Jesus always shows me grace, stops me before I run too far, encourages me and then places me back on the right path going in the right direction.

Challenge:

Take a chance on Jesus and allow Him to be your best friend, your brother or your husband, whichever one feels right for you, and begin hanging out together. This is the beginning of you conversing with Jesus and hearing from His heart, how much He loves you and desires to court you. I realize this is easier to do for women than men. For my men reading this, see yourself as a child and approach Jesus from that place instead of as your adult self. Let Him be that perfect best friend or older brother for you if that is safe.

If you are willing to get even more uncomfortable for Jesus, begin by sitting down with a pen and notebook and ask Him; *What do you think about me?* How do you see me? *Is there a lie I have believed about you?* Write down the first thing you hear or see. Don't second guess yourself. Be like a child and ask questions. Be inquisitive. Jesus wants to connect and be in a relationship with you. Remember, in order to form any relationship, you need to take time getting to know that person and you need to communicate back and forth.

I want to encourage and challenge you to go deeper each day, asking questions about what you hear and see. Be intentional practicing not knowing and asking questions. I pray that you eventually have a crush on Jesus and this crush will then lead to falling madly in love with Him. He is already madly in love with you. We are the ones that need to see His desire for us in order to reciprocate. Allow your one-on-one dates with Jesus to grow in quantity and quality. As this happens, you will begin to not only view Jesus differently but yourself too. I began to love myself and as this happened, my need for acceptance and approval from the outside world began to diminish as my need for Jesus increased.

If like me, you have struggled with an unhealthy need to be noticed, approved of, accepted and desired by the opposite sex, or same sex. My advice to you is to begin by taking at least a year off from dating and just allow Jesus to court you. Take care of you and find out where within you, inner healing is necessary. Take time to find out where the confusion, brokenness, emptiness or loneliness came in. You are worth it.

If you are recently separated or divorced, I encourage you to do the same because unless you repair what is broken within you, you will continue to experience broken relationships. It takes two to have a relationship, so *finger pointing will not produce wholeness within you, only humbling yourself before God will.*

"You can only fix you and until you fix you, you will continue to attract to you what has not been fixed within you."

With Father God

After a few months of getting uncomfortable with Jesus, He then reintroduced me to Father God. I say *reintroduced* because the God I knew before, was not the God Jesus knew. Jesus Himself introduced me to Him and for the first time ever, I sat in a Father's lap. At first it was very strange; mainly because I had never sat in my own dads lap so it did not feel natural to me, but I did it anyway. Ever so slowly I began trusting God too and those religious beliefs faded away. I once again pressed through the feelings of uncomfortableness to achieve comfort and yes, it happened! God soon became Father, then Dad, then Daddy and now Papa. As more lies were stripped away, my trust in Him as a good and safe God grew, as did my ability to be comfortable with intimacy. I soon was not only sitting in His lap, but I was having full on conversations with Him, leaning against Him or walking alongside Him. I became childlike in this season and this brought me into a deeper reverence and awe of God along with more inner healing and freedom. He lovingly and patiently demonstrated to me the truth about unconditional love and intimacy which dissolved all religious beliefs. It was love in its purest form, no fear or condemnation, but just His demonstration of unconditional love. This beautiful and pure, noncondemning love was the birthplace of healing me of my own father wounds.

During this courting time with Father God, I learned that the so-called fantasy and pseudo "love" I had worshipped and made my God was counterfeit and not the real love my heavenly Dad was about. Once I was introduced to the Agape love of my heavenly Father, I refused to settle for less and craved more and more. This passion within me was the driving force behind me pursuing a daily intimate connection with my heavenly Dad, just like I had experienced with Jesus during my teatime. It brought about within me a deep desire to daily choose to die of my old ways of religious thinking and false beliefs and enter a beautiful new courtship and covenant of trust, faithfulness and unconditional love.

The great news is that God has no strings attached to His love. He will not hold it over your head, play games with you or try to trick you to love Him. There is no manipulation with God because His love does not involve fear. His love is pure and will never run out. For the first time I knew this truth deep down and in addition realized that no person or pain was worth interfering with the love God so deeply desired to lavish upon me by hanging onto unforgiveness. He chose me and I was now choosing Him too.

1 John 4:18 - There is no fear in love. But perfect love drives out fear, because fear has to do with punishment. The one who fears is not made perfect in love.

The above verse is one I must repeatedly remind myself of due to the level of fear I experienced while growing up and how love was demonstrated to me. As I became more intimate with God as my dad, friend, provider and protector, I began discovering just how messed up my thinking had been all those years as I viewed Him instead as angry and as a punisher. I feared Him but not from a place of reverence and awe, but as someone displeased with me and out to get me.

As I developed a relationship with God not based in religion but in friendship, reverence and awe, my old ways of thinking began to change and the old perspectives I once had were replaced by truth. I also realized that since I had been raised in fear, I lived life in survival mode most of the time which also showed me that I truly was not understanding or experiencing His perfect love since it casts out all fear. I had to relearn from His heart, not mans what perfect love looked like and why I was so uncomfortable with it. As fear would emerge in my thinking, I would not succumb to it but instead I would remind myself of the above verse and that God is my protector so there was nothing to fear. Slowly, fear crept in less and less and I was becoming more comfortable with receiving and demonstrating love.

Other Glorious Names of God and their meanings

El Shaddai – Lord God Almighty

El Elyon – The Most High God

Adonai – Lord, Master

Yahweh – Lord, Jehovah

Jehovah Nissi – The Lord My Banner

Jehovah Raah – The Lord My Shepherd

Jehovah Rapha – The Lord that Heals

Jehovah Shammah – The Lord is There

Elohim – God

El Olam – The Everlasting God

Jehovah Jireh – The Lord will Provide

Jehovah Sabaoth – The Lord of Hosts

Jehovah Shalom – The Lord is Peace

Jehovah Mekoddishkem – The Lord who Sanctifies you

Jehovah Tsidkenu – The Lord Our Righteousness

Challenge:

Repeat the challenge written in the above section with Jesus. Sit down with God, possibly in His lap if you are willing and ask Him the same questions you asked Jesus; *What do you think of me? How do you see me? Are there any lies I am believing about you?* Begin with these questions and as you feel more comfortable, expand asking Him whatever your heart desires to ask. Once again, write everything down. What you see, feel and hear. Do not leave anything out.

With Holy Spirit

Through all these seasons of new discovery, inner transformation and restoration, Holy Spirit came alongside and instructed, nurtured, comforted and counseled me into wisdom and truth. Holy Spirit and I too became best of friends and with His impartations and spiritual wisdom; I was able to spiritually enter supernatural experiences that transformed me from the inside out.

Together, we went after walls, strongholds, lies, curses, hexes, false belief systems, soul ties and anything else He revealed to me that needed to be dealt with. During this new journey from death to life, darkness to light and experiencing new heights of supernatural wonder and awe, I discovered and uncovered so many truths and hidden treasures of heaven and the pure and very real love of my heavenly family. The intentions of God, Jesus and Holy Spirit was to strip away more and more layers of my old self so I could see, hear and feel an increase of their perspective and presence, and it worked.

I have to say that I absolutely love my time with Holy Spirit. He has such a great sense of humor, keeps me laughing and on my toes. He challenges me when I need to be challenged, corrects me when necessary and goofs off when He knows I have had enough schooling and stretching for one day. He has been with God since the beginning and knows everything. The Holy Spirit is and has always been a lifeline to God the Father and Jesus. The more we learn about the Holy Spirit the more we learn about God and Jesus because the three are one.

Genesis 1:2 - Now the earth was formless and empty, darkness was over the surface of the deep, and the Spirit of God was hovering over the waters.

It is the power of the Holy Spirit that produces within me the drive and desire to pursue higher levels of supernatural connection with God and heaven above. Jesus recognized the importance of Holy Spirit which is why He told His disciples that it was best that He go. He knew that once Pentecost happened in the upper room and they became filled with the power of the Holy Spirit, then and only then would they be able to demonstrate the miracles, signs and wonders that Jesus Himself demonstrated while alive. Without the presence and power of The Holy Spirit, there is no way to release the presence of heaven or activate the power of heaven within you. I highly encourage you to get to know The Holy Spirit; He is real, is not scary and is here for you.

As I walked on this journey alongside Holy Spirit, He continually blessed me with spiritual gifts of healing, discernment, tongues, knowledge, understanding, wisdom, prophecy, interpretation of tongues, faith, dreams and visions. As I pursued, He met me; as I asked, He answered; as I hungered, He fed me and as I thirst for more, He gave me plenty to drink. I pray that you will not be fearful of His presence or intimidated by what He represents. I pray that what you might have heard about Holy Spirit from a pulpit will not sway you negatively where you resist encountering Him or engaging His presence. I encourage you to challenge yourself and take a chance; I believe you will be glad you did.

John 3: 5 - Jesus answered, "Very truly I tell you, no one can enter the kingdom of God unless they are born of water and the Spirit.

Bible Facts:

The term **Holy Spirit** *appears at least 90 times in the New Testament. The sacredness of the Holy Spirit to Christians is affirmed in all three Gospels (Matthew 12:30–32, Mark 3:28–30 and Luke 12:8–10) which proclaim that* **blasphemy** *against* **The Holy Spirit** *is the* **unforgivable sin.**

Matthew 12:30-32NIV - Whoever is not with me is against me, and whoever does not gather with me scatters. And so I tell you, every kind of sin and slander can be forgiven, but blasphemy against the Spirit will not be forgiven. Anyone who speaks a word against the Son of Man will be forgiven, but anyone who speaks against the Holy Spirit will not be forgiven, either in this age or in the age to come.

- *There are nine (9)* **fruits The Holy Spirit** *produces, and they are: love, joy, peace, patience, kindness, goodness, faithfulness, humility, and self-control.*

Galatians 5:22-23 NIV - But the fruit of the Spirit is love, joy, peace, forbearance, kindness, goodness, faithfulness, gentleness and self-control. Against such things there is no law.

- *There are nine (9)* **gifts of The Holy Spirit** *and they are: wisdom, knowledge, faith, healing, miracles, prophesy, discernment of spirits, tongues, interpretation of tongues.*

1 Corinthians 12: 7-11 NIV Now to each one the manifestation of the Spirit is given for the common good. To one there is given through the Spirit a message of wisdom, to another a message of knowledge by means of the same Spirit, to another faith by the same Spirit, to another gifts of healing by that one Spirit, to

another miraculous powers, to another prophecy, to another distinguishing between spirits, to another speaking in different kinds of tongues, and to still another the interpretation of tongues. All these are the work of one and the same Spirit, and he distributes them to each one, just as he determines.

There are 9 fruits and 9 gifts of The Holy Spirit and the biblical meaning behind the number 9 is - a symbol of completeness of God and a symbol of finality. It means that God completed his creation and all his promises.

- *Other names mentioned in Scripture to describe **The Holy Spirit** are: **Dove, Comforter, Intercessor, Paraclete, Presence of God, Spirit, Spirit of God, Spirit of Truth, Helper, and Counselor.***

Engaging with All Three

Ecclesiastes 4:12 - Though one may be overpowered, two can defend themselves. A cord of three strands is not quickly broken.

As you continue to get uncomfortable and grow in relationship with God, Jesus and Holy Spirit; as you begin discovering your authentic identity and what they say about you; as you grow in confidence because you finally begin to realize your true worth, value and purpose, and as you begin to accept and see yourself as a son and daughter of God rather than a slave, victim or orphan, you will desire to take better care of your spiritual needs. The ways and importance of the world will no longer matter and a newfound desire to please God alone resonates from deep within.

I see it like an echo, as God calls out to your spirit the truths about what He says about you, your spirit will come alive and echo back.

You will soar to new heights like the eagle that you never thought was possible. It is something that I cannot completely explain but it happens. As I spent more intimate time with all three of them, and as they gently removed layer upon layer of pain from within and around my heart, they always replaced each layer with additional inner transformational healing through truth, and the pain that once fed me and led me no longer did, and the best part was that I was completely okay with that.

To this day, I never miss the lifestyle I once chose to entertain. I never miss the nightclubs, the one night stands, the mistress roles I accepted, the mornings waking up not knowing the name of the person I just had sex with, the hangovers; since I needed to drink to feel better about what I was doing, the tears I shed when I realized what I had just done, the repeated feelings of rejection and loss as once again I was just used for a good time, the feelings of shame, self-hate and self-disgust or the tear-filled nights waiting to hear from a guy I thought cared about me or loved me. Yep, not missing it one Iota!

I no longer need the approval from people that really don't deserve that much power or importance in the first place. The more I pursued God's truth, the cleaner and clearer my mind, heart, soul and spirit became. That's the power of the three-strand cord, the power of the cross and the power of His redeeming love. When you invite God, Jesus and Holy Spirit into your healing process; transformation is inevitable and life altering to say the least.

Here are just a few things I have experienced first-hand from partnering with the healing guidance of my heavenly trio.

- You will begin to heal from past emotional wounds.
- You will grow a conscious and things will change.

- You will begin desiring more connection and deeper intimacy with all three.
- Your flesh will begin taking a backseat.
- Your previous life will literally be in the past where it belongs.
- Your perspective will change, and you will begin seeing things differently.
- You will become more aware of the nudging by Holy Spirit to make other adjustments as well.
- You will be open, willing and ready for additional fine tuning and change.
- You will experience more peace, joy and love in your life.
- You will begin walking in the fullness of the Spirit instead of the flesh.
- His word will begin coming to life within you.
- You will begin discovering the true meaning of unconditional love.
- Scripture verses will come to life and you will desire this form of wisdom.

To just say that everything changed in my life is an understatement. I began seeing, hearing and experiencing life completely different. The more time I spent openly communicating with God, Jesus and Holy Spirit, the more layers of dirt were removed from my heart, my eyes, my ears, my spirit and soul. I began noticing the beauty around me. The colors of the sky, trees and flowers even became brighter and I took notice of them for the first time. My attention was off myself and onto the blessings around me. It was as if I had been blind and deaf and now could see and hear again.

Free to Be Me

Since my encounter that night in 2012, God has been on a mission to catch me up where He needed to spiritually and emotionally with all the years I had spent in the wilderness. I was His prodigal daughter and He was celebrating my return and now protecting me from further harm. I am humbly grateful for His grace, mercy and relentless pursuit of me through even my times of darkness. His ongoing demonstration of unconditional love meant the world to me. I had been so consumed in the past with my own feelings of rejection and misfortune that I had never looked beyond it to see God's hand outstretched towards me and now that I am aware of it, I am never letting go.

That lonely and very painful night in 2012, I was filled with intense grief and death but today, God has replaced all of it with joy, hope and internal freedom. I can say with certainty that I would never have left my path of going around my mountain of sexual sin and counterfeit love if I would not have stopped, died to myself and desired deep transformational inner healing and change. I had to want it in order to get it. I knew that for my circumstances to change around me, I needed to change deep within.

The way I had been choosing to live my life was not working and I had to humble myself to not only admit to that but be open to allowing God to have His way deep within me. I knew that day in my bedroom that I had to do everything different this time or I would be back there in another 5 years. I am not speaking of myself here from a place of pride but complete humility. It is from this passion deep within my heart for restoration and transformation that I can say with confidence today what worked and what did not. Been there, done that and I wrote the book!

That night in my bedroom, I died and came back to life. I was like a caterpillar that had to turn to liquid first before it could change into a beautiful butterfly and I too needed the struggle, so my wings would be strong enough so I could fly. What once appeared as a very lonely and scary night has instead turned out to be a transformational celebration that had been predestined to happen. I experienced a death of myself and then the birth of new life.

That moment will always be my special time at the well with Jesus, my Lazarus moment, my Abraham and Isaac moment, my Mary Magdalene moment and my touching the hem of Jesus' garment all rolled into one. It will always hold a special place in my heart because even though I was broken, Jesus saw me healed and so took it upon himself to carry me there, across the desert sand, through the deepest and darkest forests and out into the beautiful meadow where we still experience our dance of intimacy.

I am who I am today, and where I am today in connection with my Heavenly Dad, Jesus and Holy Spirit because of that encounter. I experienced firsthand just how much He loves and believes in me. He believed in me even when I did not believe in myself and boy that just blessed my socks off. I love that! He never doubted me because He already knew my future and the exact time He planned on intervening. That day was a divine intervention and today, I am so grateful for it. I can testify to His unwavering, intentional, persistent and unconditional love. Thank goodness He never gives up.

Today, as a healed, restored and transformed 56-year old woman, I welcome the tears of sorrow, hope, joy, uncomfortable challenges, stretching, pruning, refining and remolding, regardless of the temporary discomfort they might bring. I welcome the challenge knowing that through this discomfort, comfort and breakthrough lie on the other side. I no longer partner with shame, loneliness or rejection because today I stand by faith in truth, knowing that I was never alone, He never was ashamed of me, He delights in me, He chose me, and He will never leave me or forsake me. He was always there for me in the past, is here today with me and will be there in the days to come. His word is no longer just memorized verses but truth that is alive within me because He is alive within me. They are a part of me, in my DNA, my blood.

As I come to the end, the one thing I hope and pray you receive from my restoration and transformation story is that God loves you regardless of what you have or haven't done. He is a relational not religious God. He can be trusted and has your best interest in mind. I pray that you can connect with Him on a deeper, more intimate level and receive the healing for your heart, spirit and soul that Jesus so desires for you to receive. God created you for that one reason, to love and connect with you. When He sees you (and He does), He doesn't see your sin. He sees the child He adores and loves. He is a God who loves—desiring all His children; you included, *sanctified and set free.*

NOTES

NOTES

ABOUT THE AUTHOR

Rev. Marcia Ann Congdon is a Licensed Ordained Minister under the IPHC; International Pentecostal Holiness Church and SonShine Network Ministries. She founded Butterfly Blue Ministries in 2014 alongside her husband Dave, where they help guide others into the welcoming arms of Jesus so they too can discover their authentic identity and be transformed within their spirit, heart and soul. Marcia Ann has a passion for others to break free from any prison cells of shame, orphan, victim or slave so they too can experience a newfound freedom established in God's truth and guaranteed to produce life not death. She resides in Acworth, Georgia with her amazing husband, Dave, beautiful daughter, Kaitlyn and two Crazy Chihuahua's, Moose and Jel.

Made in the USA
Columbia, SC
15 February 2020